Twelve Little Ways
to Transform Your Heart

Twelve Little Ways
to Transform Your Heart

Lessons in Holiness and Evangelization
from St. Thérèse of Lisieux

Susan Muto

AVE MARIA PRESS AVE Notre Dame, Indiana

© 2016 by Susan Muto

Foreword © 2016 by Mike Aquilina

All rights reserved. No part of this book may be used or reproduced in any manner whatsoever, except in the case of reprints in the context of reviews, without written permission from Ave Maria Press®, Inc., P.O. Box 428, Notre Dame, IN 46556, 1-800-282-1865.

Founded in 1865, Ave Maria Press is a ministry of the United States Province of Holy Cross.

www.avemariapress.com

Paperback: ISBN-13 978-1-59471-667-6

E-book: ISBN-13 978-1-59471-668-3

Cover image "St. Thérèse of Lisieux" © Sue Kouma Johnson, SueKoumaJohnson.com. Available at the Tree of Heaven shop on etsy.com.

Cover and text design by Andy Wagoner.

Printed and bound in the United States of America.

Library of Congress Cataloging-in-Publication Data

Names: Muto, Susan, 1942- author.

Title: Twelve little ways to transform your heart : lessons in holiness and evangelization from St. Thérèse of Lisieux / Susan Muto.

Description: Notre Dame, Indiana : Ave Maria Press, 2016. | Includes bibliographical references.

Identifiers: LCCN 2016017999 (print) | LCCN 2016023832 (ebook) | ISBN 9781594716676 | ISBN 1594716676 | ISBN 9781594716683 () | ISBN 1594716684 ()

Subjects: LCSH: Thérèse, de Lisieux, Saint, 1873-1897. | Christian life--Catholic authors.

Classification: LCC BX4700.T5 M88 2016 (print) | LCC BX4700.T5 (ebook) | DDC 248.4--dc23

LC record available at https://lccn.loc.gov/2016017999

*To the staff and students
of the Epiphany Academy,
who live every day
in love and service
of the Lord.*

Is the atom a small thing?
And yet what havoc it has wrought.
Is her little way a small
contribution to the life of the Spirit?
It has all the power of the
Spirit of Christianity behind it.
It is an explosive force that can
transform our lives and the
life of the world, once put into effect.

—Dorothy Day

Contents

Foreword

The poet Samuel Hazo speaks of Susan Muto as "the one that got away."

He means it not in any romantic sense—Sam is a man married happily, to the point of ecstasy—but as part of his singular mission and passion in life: the practice and promotion of poetry. His graduate student Susan Muto understood poetry in a profound and intuitive way—she was working on a dissertation on John Milton—and she communicated her understanding with the clarity of spring water. Sam intended to offer her a job with his fledgling International Poetry Forum. Susan, he believed, would be a key to its success.

But Spiritan father Adrian van Kaam got to Susan first. And the rest, as they say, is history—or, to put it more precisely, it's formative spirituality.

Sam Hazo lost this one *not* because he was competing with a brilliant Dutch priest. He lost because he was competing with God.

What Susan Muto got, when she showed up for an interview with Fr. van Kaam, was not a job; it was a calling. It was the calling that led to this book.

I don't know anyone more qualified to write a book about power of the Little Way to transform hearts.

Susan has accomplished big things in life. In the generation after the Second Vatican Council, she emerged as a leading voice in the development of Catholic spirituality. She wrote dozens of books and hundreds of articles. She lectured tirelessly. She edited three journals and cofounded an institute. In all her work, she strove to translate the great tradition of spirituality into terms that a new generation could understand—a generation disoriented by the pace of technological progress, dislocated by wars, and traumatized by the suddenness of change.

Despite her astonishing success, Susan Muto's work has never been about Susan Muto. She has accomplished big things, but in a true Little Way. She has devoted herself to the vision and genius of her mentor, Fr. van Kaam. She commits herself to a mission. She holds herself accountable to a tradition. She serves the Church.

I travel a lot for my work, and I do a lot of public speaking, but I love the city I call my home, and I usually find a way to express my love for Pittsburgh. I cannot tell you how many times people have come up to me and said: "You're from Pittsburgh; do you know Susan Muto?" And I can predict the line that inevitably comes next: "Her work healed me."

It pleases me that Susan's healing work will reach still more people through this book. I consider it a singular honor to be asked to recommend it. Poetry's loss is the great gain of anyone, now, who wishes to live with a true life of loving prayer.

Mike Aquilina

Preface

Having been born and bred in Pittsburgh, Pennsylvania, I find it impossible to travel through a tunnel or over a bridge to a school or church where I am to speak without someone looking over the directions and immediately informing me, "But I know a shortcut." There is hardly any place in this city of rolling hills and ethnic neighborhoods that cannot be accessed by a shortcut.

Perhaps this memory explains why I found St. Thérèse's delight when she compared the new invention of an elevator to her finding a shortcut to heaven so charming. She names the latter "the little way of spiritual childhood," which is the inspiration for this book.

We live in an era where complexity often trumps simplicity. Churches and schools are inundated with more information-based programs that promise to enhance the faith. Producers vie to sell computer systems guaranteed to give staffs more time—only to end up cramping already tight schedules with complex learning curves.

At this stage of my ministry, I find myself leaning toward virtues like clarity and practices like opening one's heart to the leading of the Holy Spirit and allowing more, not less, time for prayer, meditative reflection, and formative reading.

I grew up with the philosophy that small is beautiful. As a typical Italian American blue-collar family, we focused on what we needed—a clean, homey place to live, good, mostly fresh-from-the-garden food on the table, and time to enjoy family gatherings without the interference of frenetic attachments to social media. When I wrote my book *Table of Plenty* (2014), I returned to the stories and recipes that filled my early life at home. There I enjoyed a simple but solid Christian upbringing where seeds of love and service were planted in my heart and where I saw evidence, especially in my parents, of their blooming.

When I went from high school to graduate studies, I became the first woman in my immediate family to pursue a doctorate. My specialty was post-reformation spirituality represented, among others, by the Anglican poet T. S. Eliot. I studied in particular his edifying masterpiece *Four Quartets*. There I discovered the spiritual writer he credits with influencing him, the sixteenth-century master of ascetical-mystical theology, St. John of the Cross. At a relatively young age, I delved into his *Collected Works*, knowing that it would take a lifetime to grasp the whole truth of discipleship he lived and taught. From there I found my way to the writings of St. Teresa of Avila and later those of St. Thérèse of Lisieux and other Carmelite mystics closer to our time, like St. Edith Stein. Through my academic work, first at Duquesne University and later at the Epiphany Academy of Formative Spirituality, cofounded with Fr. Adrian van Kaam (1920–2007), I challenged myself to reclaim the two-thousand-year treasury of the ancient, medieval, and modern masters of human and Christian formation. I felt drawn to Carmelite spirituality, especially the poetry of St. John of the Cross and the autobiographical writings of "Big Teresa" and "Little Thérèse," who inspired me to ponder in as clear and simple a way as possible the Church's call to the New Evangelization.

The Gospel was to be lived daily by average people in the pew like myself. There had to be a way to follow Jesus and to fulfill my vocation as a single person in the world.

Thérèse would be the one to help me reach this Christian formation ideal. Hers, like mine, was a "mustard seed" theology. It did not take much to walk in the footsteps of the Lord: a pinch of salt, a small measure of yeast, a place among the little flock.

In addition to the many books I have written myself and coauthored with Fr. Adrian, there was an urgency in me to write this book now in service of adult faith formation. I felt obliged to distinguish it from more information about the faith. This book almost begged to be written: twelve little ways to transform our hearts and in turn to change our world; to learn the lessons of evangelization from a gentle, joyful Doctor of the Church, who intuited what I and others needed to do to resist the glamour of the spectacular and reclaim the richness of the ordinary; to return to the simplicity and beauty of the sacramental life; to increase our friendship with the Lord and hence to be found worthy to befriend others in his name.

I have learned more lessons from this journey with Thérèse than I can count, not the least of which is her "ministry of the smile." It was a lesson embodied throughout his life by Fr. Adrian van Kaam. Toward the end of his earthly sojourn, when he was under the care of the Little Sisters of the Poor due to his infirmity, he lost energy, stamina, and the power of speech, but not his smile. Little did he know how much evangelizing work he did without using any words at all. His caregivers would meet me at the door of the sisters' facility in Pittsburgh and tell me over and over again, "Dr. Muto, we live for Fr. Adrian's smile."

This was for me an example of doing the work of evangelization with all of the joy and simplicity of which

Pope Francis himself speaks. Thank you, dear Thérèse, for showing me, and so many others, that there are *twelve* little ways to enter into the apostolic work, worship, and witness that must be accomplished by all of us to advance the reign of God on earth.

Introduction

The Two Childhoods of Thérèse of Lisieux

If a child is to cherish his mother,
She has to cry with him and share his sorrows.
O my dearest Mother, on this foreign shore
How many tears you shed to draw me to you!
"Why I Love You, O Mary"[1]

My faith, like yours, has grown deeper than I could have imagined when I made my First Holy Communion or received the sacrament of Confirmation. At that time, 1954 to be exact, the choice of one's Confirmation name was a central part of the instruction we received from the sisters in our grade school. Was there a saint we admired like Lucy, protector of eyesight, or Monica, exemplar of motherhood? The sister in charge of religion classes made sure we were familiar with the lives of the saints.

No matter how many I came to know, none of their names seemed right for me. That dilemma ended during the Lenten season when my classmates and I participated in the living Stations of the Cross. When we came to the sixth one—the depiction of Veronica wiping the face of Jesus—I had my name! She was courageous. She wanted to relieve the suffering of her Savior by cleansing the sweat and blood from his brow. She was an icon of truth.

1

The more I got to know her, the more I realized that God had touched my heart the way Veronica had placed her tender hands on his torn face.

God would never be for me an impersonal force setting the cosmos in motion and then leaving us to our own devices. God is Emmanuel. My Lord is Brother, Friend, Spouse, Good Shepherd, Savior. I treasure our relationship so much that I want it to enter into the pedestrian demands and details of daily life. I long to experience persons, events, and things in the light of God's love and to offer that gift of unconditional acceptance to others. When I speak, write, and teach, I want listeners, readers, and students to let the Christ in me meet and greet the Christ in them. I want to be more conscious than ever of the need to grow in faith, hope, and love and to let the joy of the Gospel fill my heart.

When I kneel before the Blessed Sacrament, I try to envision the day when all of us will become the new evangelizers the Church needs us to be in the third millennium of Christianity. To the question of how could this transformation happen, the answer is clear: "nothing will be impossible with God" (Lk 1:37).

The inspiration for this book is one of the greatest evangelizers in the Body of Christ: Thérèse of Lisieux (1873–1897), a Carmelite nun, a saint, and a Doctor of the universal Church. Though she died of tuberculosis at the age of twenty-four, she became a sanctifying force in the ecclesial world and a model for its missionary endeavors. This journey began, as it begins with all of us, from the hearth of our childhood—in this case, in the home of Louis and Zelie Martin, the parents of Thérèse, whose October

2015 canonization reminds us that holiness is not just for the cloistered and clergy, but for everyone.

Early Lessons in Love: St. Thérèse's First Childhood

Married in 1858, Louis and Zelie had nine children, four of whom died in infancy. Of the five daughters who survived, all entered religious life. After Zelie died of cancer in 1877, at the age of forty-five, Thérèse was taken in hand by her "little mothers," her sisters Pauline and Celine, both of whom were Carmelites at Lisieux. Though Zelie and Thérèse were separated in the early years of the little girl's life due to her mother's weak condition, Thérèse wanted nothing more than to be continually at her mother's side. It was as if her mother taught her how to live the cross and how to die of love.

Louis, to whom Thérèse was deeply attached after her mother's death, supported her through many childhood illnesses like nervous trembling and "hallucinations," and in a sense made the ultimate sacrifice by confirming his youngest daughter's vocation to Carmel. Ten years before her own death in 1897, her father had an attack of paralysis, which recurred a year later. These sicknesses had a profound effect on Thérèse's personhood and her prayer life; they awakened her, as nothing else could, to the "agony and ecstasy" of a holy life in the world. In her father, as in her mother, she saw firsthand the ravages and radiant lights of living the paschal mystery. The year 1892 marked her father's last visit to Carmel—a parting that linked "sweet sorrow" to "naked faith" in the midnight moments of life, which, St. John of the Cross had taught her, is the only proximate means to union with God.

Beatified in 2008, Zelie and Louis are believed to be the first parents of a saint so honored by the Church. Their canonization in October 2015 highlighted the exemplary evangelical role parents play in their children's human and spiritual upbringing. It also reminds us of the virtue of humility; through their example, their daughters were deeply impressed with the idea that we possess nothing. Naked we come into this world and naked we leave it, for it is in God that "we live and move and have our being" (Acts 17:28). Far from grieving over her many imperfections, Thérèse took comfort in them. She considered God's greatest favor to be the revelation of her nothingness, of her incapacity to do any good by herself alone. It was this revelation that led to her "second childhood," in which she strove to become as little as possible so that God might lift her up.

Faults, says Thérèse, serve to instruct us on the way to spiritual maturity. Little ones learning to walk experience unavoidable falls from time to time. When we accept with humor and humility the imperfect selves we are, we observe how swiftly God rushes to our aid. Thérèse loves her limits because they keep her humble. She sees them as blessings in disguise because they compel her to seek the support of Jesus and the grace he imparts. We find our happiness, as Thérèse did, through accepting our littleness, having humble confidence in God's strength, and by denying ourselves for the sake of serving others. Only when we descend into our misery can we ascend to the waiting arms of Divine Mercy.

Throughout her short life, Thérèse embodied this little way, having tremendous confidence in the God in whose name she did "little things with great love." *The Story of a*

Soul, a collection of her autobiographical memoirs printed and distributed a year after her death, has never gone out of print. Beatified in 1923 and canonized in 1925, she was declared co-patron of the missions with Francis Xavier in 1927 and named copatron of France with Joan of Arc in 1944. In October of 1997, St. John Paul II declared her the thirty-third Doctor of the Church, the youngest person and the third woman to be so honored.

In addition to her autobiography, Thérèse left a library of spiritual writings, including letters, poems, religious plays, prayers, and her last conversations. At the age of three, she already had an inkling that she would be a religious and that she would refuse nothing that God asked of her. After Midnight Mass on December 25, 1886, at the age of thirteen, she experienced the grace of a second conversion, enabling her to go to Christ with complete confidence and love. In the ten years she spent as a Carmelite, she embraced a gentle lifestyle, overcame discouragement, practiced inner and outer silence, and showed the strength needed to endure terminal illness. She trusted that Jesus heard her prayers in this life and would continue to do so in the next. When she died on September 30, 1897, she promised to spend her heaven doing good on earth, a promise many say she has kept to the full.

Answering the Call: A Second Childhood

According to Thérèse, everyday life is the best arena in which to respond to the call to holiness, which is best approached from a posture of "littleness," acknowledging in humility that we ourselves possess nothing and that everything comes to us from God. Spiritual childhood implies a willingness to be small so that we can be lifted up by God. No matter what apostolate we must fulfill, it will be efficacious to the degree that we acknowledge and accept our indigence before God.

Let me pause to remember the woman who had the greatest influence on my life of faith. She was my maternal grandmother, Elizabeth, who emigrated from southern Italy to the United States at the tender age of sixteen. She was and remained illiterate, though she had the gift of reading hearts and seeing the face of Jesus in everyone she met. She entered into an arranged marriage, bore eleven children, five of whom died early of untreatable contagious diseases. With each painful relinquishment, she grew closer to God. I only knew her for the first thirteen years of my life, but Elizabeth's wit and dignity, despite great poverty, was like a breath of fresh air to everyone who enjoyed her excellent cooking and the hospitality of her table. The "breath prayer" that never left her lips and that etched itself on my heart was "O Dio mio" ("O my God"). She exemplified the way of spiritual childhood though she never read the writings of St. Thérèse of Lisieux.

Like Elizabeth, my heaven-sent grandmother, Thérèse's attractiveness also resided in the fact that she taught what she lived and lived what she taught. In her autobiography, she describes, for example, the sense of her own helplessness when she received the assignment to serve as mistress of novices:

> Lord, I am too little to nourish your children; if you wish to give through me what is suitable for each, fill my little hand and without leaving Your arms or turning my head, I shall give Your treasures to the soul who will come and ask for nourishment.[2]

Thérèse realized that the Church is a Mystical Body composed of diverse cells or members inspired and enlivened by the Holy Spirit. In this light, she was able to clarify her own vocation: since love is everything and contains all vocations, she could aspire to love and then inspire others to see it as the foundation of all other apostolic labors and vocations:

> Yes, I have my place in the Church and it is You, O my God, who have given me this place; in the heart of the Church, my Mother, I shall be Love. Thus I shall be everything, and thus my dream will be realized.[3]

This self-communication of God to her never fails to fill us with wonder. God chose a cloistered nun, who lived a regimented life of prayer and work and died in an obscure French village, to bring an infinite number of souls to Jesus. Thousands upon thousands streamed into churches to venerate her relics. What was her secret? Is it possible for us to learn what it was and then to live it in this century where secularistic forces strive to crush true Christianity? A fresh look at her life reveals that embedded in Thérèse's understanding of discipleship is the unique charism she identifies as the little way of spiritual childhood.

To be little personally means to be humble spiritually. It is to acknowledge that all of life falls under the eternally benevolent glance of God. However long we live, we still remain little children to whom the kingdom of heaven belongs (see Lk 18:17).

Fascinated though we may be by everything spectacular, Thérèse adopts the paradoxical reality that lasting glitter comes from littleness, that true riches can only be found in poverty of spirit, and that in every obstacle God discloses a formation opportunity. Implanted by God in the soil of Thérèse's littleness were the seeds of holiness that would enable her to go to heaven by a way that was straight, short, and totally new. Her compass would be the Cross, together with holy scripture, notably the epistles of St. Paul, and the writings of spiritual masters like Thomas à Kempis and John of the Cross. They taught her to practice patience and to be long-suffering in trials and to trust that the witness of her care for souls would edify countless believers and sincere seekers beyond her convent walls. So strong was God's redemptive love that it flowed through her like an unimpeded river and removed every fear of failure. In one of her poems, "The Eternal Canticle Sung in Exile," she wrote:

> My beloved, beauty supreme
> You give yourself to me,
> But in return,
> Jesus, I love you
> And my life is but one act of love![4]

If we are to go and teach the nations (see Mt 28:16–20), in fulfillment of the Great Commission Jesus gave to his disciples, it would behoove us to turn to Thérèse for the counsels we need to succeed, starting with the revealed truth that "perfect love casts out fear" (1 Jn 4:18). She shows us that the way we are to follow is neither difficult nor dramatic. Although there are evangelizers among us who receive notoriety, most of us go through life unnoticed. What comforts us when we turn to this Doctor of the Church is that she, too, lived the hidden life of Jesus of Nazareth. Like her we try our best to mirror in the mundane the remarkable power of his saving love for souls. Every time parents take their children into church rather than dropping them off at the door, they witness to what it means to be "God's chosen ones, holy and beloved, [clothed] . . . with compassion, kindness, humility, meekness, and patience" (Col 3:12). They are hidden in Christ as Christ is hidden in God (see Col 3:3). He is with them when they gather the family around the table for dinner, help youngsters with their homework, express hope for their future, and make time in their busy schedules for having fun together.

This book is not a biography of Thérèse nor is it a commentary on Carmelite spirituality. Its aim is to develop twelve facets of the little way of spiritual childhood that enhance the evangelical mission of the Church and strengthen our membership in the Body of Christ. To begin this process step by step, it is necessary to reflect on several characteristics of spiritual childhood.

• • • • •

The starting point for this pathway to spiritual maturity happens in *hiddenness* wherein we strive to initiate the hidden life of Jesus of Nazareth, growing thereby in *everyday joy* and in *trust in Divine Mercy*. These three ways prepare us to embrace the *sacramental life*; to live in *abandonment to Divine Providence* and to understand that the essence of discipleship is intimate friendship with the Lord. To follow him is to practice, as Thérèse did throughout her life, *renunciation* of our own self-will, aided by the practice of *unceasing, world-redeeming prayer*. Only then can we grow in the virtues of *simplicity* and *freedom*, gifts that characterize the children of God. These ways prepare us to follow for a lifetime the traditional threefold path of *purgation, illumination,* and *union*, thereby preparing us, as God wills, for *living in, with, and through the Lord in a martyrdom of love*.

Characteristics of Bold and Holy Love

Thérèse left everything in God's hands without holding anything in reserve. Her spirit of poverty allowed her to trust in God so much that the demons of doubt, discouragement, and distress fled from her soul. Her intention was to stand firm in spirit, however weakened her bodily functions were. In physical debilitation as well as in spiritual dryness, faith was her unfailing support. Her threefold formula for holiness—abandon yourself to God; acknowledge your nothingness; make room in your heart for God to initiate what needs to be done—perfectly describes the "second childhood" to which we all have been called. Liturgy, Word, and sacrament; private and communal worship; rituals, devotions, and traditions—all these practices protected her, as they protect us, from sentimental emotionalism on one hand or excessive activism on the other. God accomplished in Thérèse what she could never have done on her own. He showed her that self-love is as debilitating as self-loathing. He bolstered her acceptance of her indigence, replacing craven fear with holy boldness.

Thérèse's love for God, self, and others reveals several characteristics we ought to emulate in this era of the New Evangelization.

- A love that is *all-encompassing*. Thérèse vows to give her all to Jesus.

- A love that is *disinterested*, utterly selfless. Thérèse loves God solely for who he is in himself. Since God alone is our reward, we can thank him for any favors or consolations he grants while not clinging to them as ends in themselves.

- A love that is *discrete*. Discretion enabled Thérèse to hide her sufferings for fear that she might call too much attention to herself rather than pointing to God as the source of all good.

- A love that expresses itself in *simplicity*. In prayer, Thérèse told Jesus how much she loved him and desired to do his will. She did not spend a lot of time explaining to God this or that intention or action; rather, she turned to simple petitions like, "Draw me."

- A love that is *at peace*. One commitment she made was to look only at the virtues of her sisters, not at their imperfections. She sensed that focusing on faults would disturb both her personal and her communal peace. She had a horror of quarrels and preferred to let others have their say whether or not she agreed with them. When trouble arose in the community, it was her choice to be a peacemaker, capable of animating sad hearts with the joy of her smile.

- A love marked by *penance and self-renunciation*. She chose to do even the most insignificant chores out of love. Her daily routines demanded sacrifices and self-forgetful generosity. Neither dryness of soul nor the apparent absence of God caused her to lose her equanimity. She refused to get upset by bewailing her limits. She knew that love was the best means of correcting her faults and failings and letting them bear lasting fruit.

- A love marked by inner and outer *silence*. She preferred to keep silent rather than to dwell on annoyances that disrupted her inner calm. Thérèse also avoided either verbal retorts or nonverbal gestures that might impede her from behaving charitably with courtesy. Doing so supported growth in the interior disposition not to seek her own will in anything.

For Thérèse, renunciation was the key to liberation. The more she sacrificed her childish need for attention, the freer she was to love and serve God and neighbor. Freed from slavery to self, she was free to follow her vocation to love. That is why she took advantage of any chance she had to make little sacrifices. She who loved beauty and neatness learned to esteem the oldest, most mended habits, to eat what was placed in front of her, to endure the cold, to give up her desire to read a book another sister borrowed. These kinds of mortifications allowed her to live in the spirit of abnegation most needed during her final agony, when surrender was her constant companion.

My memory now turns to my dear mentor, spiritual friend, and cofounder of the Epiphany Association, Fr. Adrian van Kaam. I feel sure that in his early twenties, when he was trapped behind enemy lines in The Hague, his home city, and had to live from August 1944 to May 1945 under Nazi occupation during the infamous Dutch Hunger Winter, he knew intimately what renunciation felt like—from having to renounce his anticipated ordination to the priesthood until after the liberation, to having to give up day after day enough food to meet even the most modest dietary needs. He and many other Dutch people were reduced to a starvation ration of four hundred calories a day. And yet, as his war journals revealed, he never felt for a moment that the Gestapo could deprive him of his inner freedom. That was Christ's gift to him and no tyrant could take it away.

In a sense, it was physical deprivation that freed him, as it did Thérèse (a saint he deeply admired) to follow his vocation to love and care for others in need not only of physical sustenance but of spiritual restoration. He had an innate aesthetic sensitivity, having grown up a streetcar's ride away from Delft, the town of the great Dutch artist, Jan Vermeer.

From his earliest youth, Fr. Adrian learned how to see beneath the ugliness of war-torn streets and devastated neighborhoods the beauty of the human spirit, as when one young soldier sliced one potato into sixteen pieces to feed a gang of underground workers. Such mortifications taught him the truth of the cross and gave him the courage to practice daily what he named "appreciative abandonment to the mystery," a central concept in the field of formative spirituality that would be his life's work.

Because she believed in God's providential plan for her life, Thérèse accepted her illness as the passageway chosen by him to bring her to eternal peace. Her decision to discover what was most pleasing to him took away the sting of death (see 1 Cor 15:55) and enabled her to offer herself to God as a victim of merciful love. This pledge was not a passing act of devotion but the essence of her evangelical existence. This oblation represented her way of corresponding perfectly to the Divine Will and of rejoicing over God's entrance into her abandoned heart: "Then little children were brought to him in order that he might lay his hands on them and pray. The disciples spoke sternly to those who brought them; but Jesus said, 'Let the little children come to me, and do not stop them; for it is to such as these that the kingdom of heaven belongs'" (Mt 19:13–14).

To begin a journey implies that we have in mind a destination we want to reach. Despite the detours we may take along the way, the goal of spiritual childhood is to abandon oneself without reservation to God: "Jesus deigned to show me the road that leads to this Divine Furnace, and this road is the *surrender* of the little child who sleeps without fear in its Father's arms."[5]

The desire for sacrificial commitment filled Thérèse's spirit, but bodily weakness made it impossible for her to seek a missionary vocation in foreign lands. What then was she called to do? Through reflection on the scriptures and on her own experience, she found that the way to resolve this dilemma was to become love in the heart of the Church.

As long as she exercised this will-to-love to the highest possible degree, Thérèse had every confidence that "God would transform this ember of her 'nothingness' into *fire*."[6] Once she opened her heart to the gift of Christ's peace, old doubts fled, leaving her with the conviction that suffering with joy wins souls for Christ and releases favors of grace beyond what she could have imagined. Her response to this evangelical call was to make an act of oblation to merciful love, which she tried to do in the most exemplary manner possible:

> O my God! Most Blessed Trinity, I desire to *love* You and make You *loved*, to work for the glory of Holy Church by saving souls on earth and of liberating those suffering in purgatory. I desire to accomplish Your will perfectly and to reach the degree of glory You have prepared for me in Your Kingdom. I desire, in a word, to be a saint, but I feel my helplessness and I beg You, O my God! to be Yourself my *Sanctity*! Since You loved me so much as to give me Your only Son as my Savior and my Spouse,

the infinite treasures of His merits are mine. I offer them
to You with gladness, begging You to look upon me only
in the Face of Jesus and His heart burning with *Love*.[7]

Though she herself had only a few more years to live before
consumption took its toll, Thérèse taught her sisters, the
novices under her charge, and all those who embraced
her "little way" how to live a life of joyful abandonment
to Divine Providence. They, too, ought to try to turn the
smallest events into occasions of grace and the darkest trials of suffering into times of mystical transformation.

This is a lesson every disciple of Christ can and must
learn. In each of our lives there are numerous seemingly
innocuous happenings that are openings to God's always
outpouring grace. Loading the dishwasher, who knows
how often now, becomes an invitation to see each dish as
a symbol of what you and your loved ones need to sustain
life. While soaking soiled laundry, you thank God for each
body this or that piece of clothing comforts.

In the way of spiritual childhood, the more these practices are done with love, the more they become a segue
to spiritual significance. It brings joy to the most ordinary
day and readies you to face the far more difficult challenge
of connecting human misery with an unshakeable conviction of God's mercy.

What sustained Thérèse through her own nights of
faith as well as through the small annoyances she encountered daily was her willingness "to make a prayer of suffering."[8] One of her favorites became, *"Draw me* and *we
shall run."* It saw her through spells of near suffocation,
the vomiting of blood, and a high fever. Until the hour of
her death, she managed with the help of God to maintain
her ministry of the smile. It was her way of showing trust,

acceptance, and absolute surrender—all characteristics of a sacrificial victim witnessing to Christ's redemptive love and the salvation of souls.

1

The Little Way of Hiddenness

Ah! Lord, let me hide in your Face,
There I'll no longer hear the world's vain noise,
Give me your love, keep me in your grace
Just for today.
"My Song for Today"[1]

As it is commonly understood, "evangelizing" is something done as a public event, often in stadiums, where seekers hear an altar call and come to Jesus; on television and radio stations where dynamic speakers tell the story of their conversion; and in megachurches where hundreds gather to praise the Lord.

I felt the full force of this kind of evangelizing in a "rally for Jesus" event I attended when I was in college. The enthusiasm of everyone around me was irresistible. Jesus was there in music, song, and liturgical dance. It was not easy to leave this mountaintop experience and return to my local parish, but it had to be done.

That is why to place evangelization in the context of the hidden life seems at first glance to be a contradiction in terms. And yet, is this not where Jesus himself began his ministry? Turning to the Gospel of Luke, we meet him as a boy of twelve teaching in the temple after which we

17

are told he rejoined his mother Mary and his foster father, Joseph, went with them to Nazareth and was obedient to them (see Lk 2:51). Between that time and his reappearance at his baptism around the age of thirty (see Lk 3:23), Jesus led a hidden life. All we know is that he increased in wisdom, in age, and in divine and human favor (see Lk 2:52).These years of obscurity do not preclude evangelization; instead they provide its preparatory ground.

There can be no doubt that Thérèse has a predilection for hiddenness. In her *Story of a Soul*, there are innumerable references to the word "hidden." From childhood onward, Thérèse trod the path of suffering. In his psychological and spiritual reflections on her life, Fr. Marc Foley, O.C.D., author of *The Context of Holiness*, reminds us that she was scarred emotionally by the death of her mother when she was only four years old; that she was bedridden as a result of a neurotic episode at the age of ten; that she struggled with debilitating scruples most of her life; and that she underwent an agonizing dark night of the senses and the spirit ending in the consumption that killed her. And yet, few people knew of these multiple nights of faith. Affliction was the hidden flower Thérèse picked for Jesus from the garden of her brief existence and from the treasures she found in the Gospels. God himself unveiled them to her as loving parents reveal the secrets of how to live a holy and happy life to their children.

Thérèse strove to be empty of self-centeredness so that she might be found worthy to be made full of God. She placed herself under the direction of God's sovereign will. Having once been the center of everyone's attention, all she wanted as a Carmelite was to hide every sign of self-absorption from others so that in her they would see

Jesus. To be a mirror of her Beloved for others meant that she had to hide away all her accumulated mental and emotional baggage and be ready at every moment to receive him in her heart.

As a child, Thérèse loved to play hide-and-seek with her sisters and their friends. It was as if she considered it to be a foretaste of what God had in store for her: "I felt that Carmel was a *desert* where God wanted me to go to hide myself."[2] She intuited that the way to serve God did not lie in the performance of striking works but in hiding ourselves from the passing glitter of vainglory. In secret, Jesus instructed her that she was to practice virtue in such a way "that the left hand knows not what the right is doing."[3]

The hidden life became for Thérèse the soil in which the Lord planted the seeds of evangelization that we are to harvest with his help over a lifetime. Self-giving, self-effacing love is the most recognizable trait shared by the Christ-centered, Gospel-oriented children of God. Because Jesus had found her in her hiding place, it was not necessary for Thérèse to devise new ways to come to Christian perfection; her path to holiness consisted of responding to the guidance of the Spirit in the mundane details of convent life. Her dependence on the Lord unlocked for Thérèse a veritable treasury of spiritual truths; it increased her ability to discern occasions for evangelical witness others might be inclined to overlook. These "little nothings" were not self-chosen but divinely initiated. They were housed in the limited but blessed circumstances of her life at Lisieux. She practiced self-abandonment to Divine Providence by witnessing to Christ when she was folding "up the mantles forgotten by the Sisters"[4] or transporting Sister St. Pierre to the refectory.[5] Doing these "little nothings" became the preparatory school that enabled Thérèse in both intention and action to carry Christ's message of redemptive love to the whole Church.

When you think about it, is not your life for the most part a series of the same kinds of "little nothings"? Who but God notices when you go to the drugstore early in the morning to pick up a prescription needed by a family member or when you take a moment on the way to work to telephone a sick friend or when you pay for a person's cup of coffee when she runs short of change?

To evangelize is not only to know the truths of our faith, its creeds and doctrines, but to cultivate the gifts of seeing needs as they arise and understanding how to become "wise as serpents and innocent as doves" (Mt 10:16). Thérèse accepted that she was too weak to perform evangelical feats in foreign missions but that she was strong enough to release through her acceptance of everyday life with its sufferings and joys the graces most needed at home and in the world as a whole.

The little way of spiritual childhood emphasizes the efficacy of hiddenness. It invites us on a daily basis to emulate the untold life of Jesus of Nazareth and to see its "nothingness" as a veritable treasury of graces. Mustard seed theology (a mite produces a mighty tree) does not preclude contact with the wider world, especially through prayer. It reveals the paradoxical reality that good deeds can abound with or without others knowing their origin. Self-emptying was the condition for Thérèse's being made full of God. By showing others that she owned nothing at all, she was able to give everything she accomplished to them as a gift from the Lord. From the voided vessel she was, she poured the fullness of God's presence into the heart of everyone she helped, from young novices to aging nuns. She proved day by day that we only excel at the work of evangelization when we make maximal room for Jesus to do what needs to be done with no egocentric interference on our part.

Remaining abandoned *to* the mystery was especially challenging since Thérèse had every reason to feel as if she had been abandoned *by* the mystery. It was as if she saw this facet of spiritual childhood as a discipline of *non-effort*, distinct from an *effort of the will*. This paradox of *effortless-effort* taught her how to let go and let God be her all in all. This exercise of non-effort flies in the face of activism; it presupposes that one allows the divine directionality to prompt one to serve others in a totally self-abandoned way. Thérèse gave herself to God in the manner of a trusting child who holds nothing but his hand in hers. She thought of herself as a little ball that Jesus could bounce around at his good pleasure. This disposition of *effortless-effort* filled the soul of this future saint with courage and confidence. She tried to go where the inspiration of the Holy Spirit led her, only to discover the truth in the Apostle Paul's claim that when we are weak, then we are strong (see 2 Cor 12:10).

By replacing will power with the will to love, Thérèse was able to accept other paradoxes coalescing in her experience. She was a child who lived in unknowing, yet she came to know the secrets of mystical love. Every obstacle she encountered in community life became an aid to her life of asceticism and mysticism. Although she used to be a pampered child fearful of suffering, now she chose the way of the cross as the aperture into which the full force of God's grace could be poured. The greater her surrender, the more initiative God took with her.

Although her illness plunged her into the midnight moment of naked faith, she declared with confidence that the sun still shone. Dense as this inner darkness was, it deepened her conviction that Christ would never abandon her. The more faults she found in herself, the surer she was of the mercy of God. The short length of her life did not matter to Jesus because it had from the beginning a sanctified purpose. She did not have time to waste in an exhausting search for human perfection; she simply had to accept her mistakes and continue to operate from the center of her humility. For example, she saw that the simpler she was the more courage she found not to complain and run away from disappointing situations. Simplicity of heart allowed her to find in every situation what God's will was. She saw that in each task she performed, Jesus wanted her to manifest his presence. Her joy was to decrease that he might increase (see Jn 3:30).

Thérèse's commitment to the hidden life of Jesus of Nazareth allowed her to perform good deeds of seemingly little consequence in secret, rather than aiming to excel in noticeable works that were forbidden to her. In her autobiography, she pens the following prayer:

> Jesus, I cannot fathom the depths of my request; I would be afraid to find myself overwhelmed under the weight of my bold desires. My excuse is that I am a *child*, and children do not reflect on the meaning of their words; however, their parents, once they are placed upon a throne and possess immense treasures, do not hesitate to satisfy the desires of the *little* ones whom they love as much as they love themselves. To please them they do foolish things, even going to the extent of becoming

weak for them. . . . The heart of a child does not seek riches and glory (even the glory of heaven). She understands that this glory belongs by right to her brothers, the angels and saints. . . . What this child asks for is Love. She knows only one thing: to love You, O Jesus. Astounding works are forbidden to her; she cannot preach the Gospel, shed her blood; but what does it matter since her brothers work in her stead and she, a *little child*, stays very close to the *throne* of the King and Queen. She *loves* in her brothers' place while they do the fighting. But how will she prove her love since love is proved by works? Well, the little child will strew flowers, she will perfume the royal throne with their sweet scents, and she will sing in her silvery tones the canticle of Love.[6]

The Holy Spirit inspired Thérèse to see that though it was impossible for her to preach the Gospel or to shed her blood, it did not matter since her brothers and sisters went to work in the world in her stead. Her chief task as a cloistered Carmelite was to stay as close as she could to Jesus—to love him in the corridors and cells of the convent while those missioned in his name fought his battles on foreign shores. She could accomplish this apostolate by seeing to it that not one sacrifice escaped her attention. She chose instead to profit from the smallest look or word she was asked to express and to do so with love. This discovery enabled her to find a way to make Jesus known and loved by all. This "fragrant shower," she said, these "fragile, worthless petals," and undoubtedly "these songs of love from the littlest heart" will *charm my Beloved*. "I will be irresistible to him and what I ask of him I am likely to receive."[7]

Every routine experience she had as a nun offered Thérèse yet another occasion to relinquish herself and to live in God. She felt no need to craft elaborate methods of prayer. It was enough to place herself in the presence of her Beloved and to cultivate continual remembrance of him. Joyful perseverance hidden from the naked eye may not be the most exciting of virtues but its staying power is undeniable.

Never will I forget the day (April 28, 1980) when Fr. Adrian van Kaam suffered an acute heart attack rendering him, as his primary care physician and our personal friend told us, in a "touch or go" state of health. It was uncertain for the first few days whether he would survive. Excellent care and round-the-clock prayer saw him through these precarious hours. What amazed me the most was that during the initial days of his recovery, he asked me to bring him a blank journal and his favorite pen. I did so the next day. When I visited him shortly thereafter, he showed me the title he had written on the cover. It was *The Blessing of a Coronary*. I knew then that he had found the courage to persevere with joy and to fulfill his calling to the best of his ability. He chose to see in this episode of physical debilitation a meaning beyond this new set of limits. Like Thérèse, he drew upon the grace that enabled him to use his suffering to benefit others. Leaving his hospital room that day, my heart swelled with gratitude. Suddenly the ordinary had become extraordinary. In this unbelievable obstacle, Fr. Adrian had found a new formation opportunity.

Aside from her awareness of the indwelling presence of the Trinity, Thérèse, like Fr. Adrian, had no special revelations or flights of ecstasy. The crux of her spirituality lay not in what she did but in the way she did it. She reached

the heights of great holiness without performing any daz-
zling feats, thereby teaching us in this era of evangelization that as long as we listen to the whispers of the Spirit
in the here-and-now situations in which we find ourselves, we will honor our call to discipleship and respond
accordingly.

Practicing mustard-seed theology as she does in all
her works, this saint and Doctor of the Church reaches the
conviction that, above all else, these "nothings" please the
Lord. Against the bane of bigness, Thérèse says it is littleness that brings "a smile to the Church Triumphant."
Flowers unpetalled in and through love will pass from
her fingers into the hands of Jesus. The fresh blooms she
gives him may have no earthly value, but they will prove
to be invaluable to the Church. Because the Father himself
has selected them, they will be invested by the Holy Spirit
with the power to gain the victory that belongs to the Son:
Thy kingdom come. Thy will be done.

In summary, there are five portals of spiritual childhood, beginning with our reclamation of the efficacy of
the hidden life. These are not the meandering thoughts of
a mystic but the instructions all of us must be willing to
follow in this era of evangelization.

The first portal to spiritual childhood is to *cultivate a
humble heart* that resists the slightest temptation to ego-in-
flation or self-absorption. Such humility results in the
overcoming of all fears and frustrations and lets us find
comfort by simply walking in the footsteps of Jesus.

The second portal is to *accept the fact of our finite, limited
existence* and derive from it a more realistic outlook on life
as wholly reliant on God.

The third portal is to *live each day with a grateful heart and to surrender to God's grace in the circumstances* in which we find ourselves.

To live detached from the need for puffed up self-importance is the fourth portal. We shun the illusory promises embedded in power, pleasure, and possession and enjoy instead the self-effacement of being who God intends us to be.

Finally, we reach the point where we can *behold in every person, event, and thing the guiding hand of Holy Providence* drawing us forth from the shadows of earthly suffering to the threshold of heavenly joy.

First Facet of the New Evangelization

To emulate the hidden life of Jesus of Nazareth in your own "Nazareths of everydayness."

Questions for Reflection

1. Can you recall a few "seeds of evangelization" you may have planted in ways unnoticed by others but nonetheless pleasing to God?

2. When you share your faith with others, do you try to root your words and deeds in the mundane details of daily life, thereby linking your evangelical accomplishments to the richness of the ordinary?

3. Can you describe an experience in your own ministerial endeavors of "effortless-effort"—when you knew that what was done was not done by you but by the grace of God?

Closing Prayer

Lord, I want to follow the way of hiddenness, in imitation of your mother Mary, but I can only do so if you grant me humility of heart and grateful surrender to your holy will. Please detach me from the paralyzing need for self-importance so that I can be an instrument of your providential care wherever you place me in suffering and in joy. Amen.

2

The Little Way of Gratitude

Grant that I may be faithful
To my divine SPOUSE Jesus.
One day may His sweet voice call me
To fly away among the elect.
Then, no more exile, no more suffering.
In Heaven I'll keep repeating
The song of my gratitude,
Lovable Queen of Carmel!
"Song of Gratitude. . . ."[1]

Most of us assume that evangelization happens from the pulpit of a dynamic preacher, and, to be sure, it often does. However, since faith is "caught before it is taught," witnessing to Gospel values is a common occurrence. If a flight incurs a long delay due to mechanical trouble, we refrain from complaining and instead engage the person next to us in a friendly conversation because it's the kind thing to do. Two people in an office cubicle decide to stop gossiping and get to know each other because it's the right thing to do. A sick person we love asks us to pray with her. At a supermarket checkout counter, we give a stranger the money he needs to complete his purchase. It's what Jesus would have done. In these ordinary circumstances, faith expands beyond those special times when we make a retreat or listen to uplifting devotional music. We need not wait for moments like this to reawaken our longing for God; we have to stay awake to the evangelizing inspirations we receive all the time.

Of all the places I could have been, I had proof of this principle in a Kmart! I had gone there in a rush to purchase a replacement part for the commode in my guest bathroom. My brother had shown me how to fix it and had assured me that the broken piece was easy to replace. The only trouble was—when I got to the store that was supposed to sell everything—the one gadget I needed was not in the plumbing department. I picked up the customer service phone, called for help, and was told a salesperson would be with me "in a minute." Finally, almost a half hour later, a woman strode toward me, not knowing how upset I felt.

Thank God, before I showed my exasperation, my eyes alighted on her nametag. It said "Irene"—a name I knew meant "peace." So instead of complaining, I asked her how she felt and expressed my concern regarding how busy her day must have been. She seemed surprised at this kindness and for the next several minutes we exchanged a few facets of life like her need to work two jobs to pay the bills, and mine to teach people in Church leadership not to grow discouraged. She apologized that what I wanted to buy was not on the shelf but assured me that it was in stock and that she could find it, and she did. Then, as we parted, I thanked her profusely. "I guess you are a follower of the Lord. You treated me with kindness and addressed me by my name as he would have done." How grateful I was that the Christ in me had met and greeted the Christ in Irene.

Thérèse had an uncanny ability to see the richness of the ordinary in everyday life. Thanks to her example, we discern the second step in the art and discipline of becoming evangelizers: to start the process on the street where we live. Here is a recently widowed woman who needs a ride to the mall. I take her out of the goodness of my heart only to realize later that she saw something of Jesus in me. Toward an obstreperous sister in the community, Thérèse acted as if she were the most agreeable person in the world. What we learn from her example is the power embedded in the *this*—a power Jesus knew so well. *This* blind man needs to see. *This* leper begs to be cleansed. *This* cripple wants to walk. *This* woman seeks forgiveness and who are we to judge her sins?

Returning to that irascible character toward which Thérèse felt no affinity, we see her ability to pierce behind a cursory glance. She sees into others as Jesus did. She preaches his Gospel in little ways that carry great significance. In *this* sister's presence, she never made aggravated sounds nor did she arouse further irritability by chastising looks. Raspy, condemnatory tones or gestures kill the effectiveness of evangelization almost immediately. What raises the bar might be a simple compliment or the thought of how holy this other person must be in the eyes of God. The enemy of evangelization is antipathy. What facilitates it is patience and the peaceful recognition that to live the Gospel takes a lifetime of learning.

The same sister who caused Thérèse to struggle so much became the recipient of her prayers. Whatever acts of love she could do for her were not a burden but a blessing.

Rather than reply to acidic remarks with more of the same, she banished from her mind bad thoughts about this nun and instead bestowed upon her her most agreeable smile.

A stance of meditative reflection lets us catch the rich undercurrent of the ordinary. We avoid facile, judgmental conclusions and discover instead the beauty of God's work of art despite some superficial flaws. Thérèse talks about practicing little virtues, little services, and little mortifications.[2] Such an appreciative stance prevents discouragement. We learn from her example that everyday evangelization does not consist in excelling in extraordinary accomplishments but in obeying God's will in the ordinary circumstances of daily life. There is no use in waiting for *the* perfect situation to witness to Christ's truth when the way he has chosen for us is before our eyes. Provided we put up no prideful resistance to God's grace, the link between our plans and God's providence will remain firm.

A synonym for "little" often used by Thérèse to highlight the richness of the ordinary is the word "simple." Thérèse never forgot the wisdom communicated to her by her superior that "the closer one approaches to God, the simpler one becomes."[3] Thérèse's way of life enables her to sidestep the temptation to dramatize the work of evangelization. Who knows how many unnoticed and unrecorded good deeds the disciples did in imitation of Christ? For every water jug made full of choice wine, there must have been hundreds of chipped cups filled with water to quench the thirst of travelers. If two fish and a few loaves of bread could feed thousands, how many meals occurred that were never recounted? It was the simplicity of her soul that enabled Thérèse to see in the Gospels "new lights, hidden and mysterious meanings."[4]

The practice of consecrating the present moment in its utter ordinariness to God was the best way not to call attention to herself. No matter where she was—in the chapel, the refectory, the infirmary—she gave glory to God, offering proof for time and eternity that silent adoration is a bridge to evangelization.

The steady practice of participatory presence to the Trinity enabled Thérèse to incarnate her love for God in her bodily, functional, and spiritual being, making her nearly delirious with joy. By no longer troubling herself about results or successes, by leaving the outcome of every deed and desire to God, she freed her mind from useless worry. She basked in the truth that "just as the sun shines simultaneously on the tall cedars and on each little flower as though it were alone on earth, so Our Lord is occupied particularly with each soul as though there were no others like it."[5] Living in presence to the Divine Presence prevented Thérèse from indulging in the throes of self-pitying introspection. Growth in self-knowledge freed her from envying those stronger than she. A complaining sourpuss would not be able to convey values of profound worth to all whom she encountered.

The Roman Catholic practice of adoration of the Blessed Sacrament speaks volumes in this regard. I find it so inspiring to go into the chapel and sit quietly with the Lord. Around me are people praying the Rosary or directing their gaze in silence at the tabernacle as if they were saying with the prophet Isaiah, "Here am I; send me!" (Is 6:8).

Thérèse's vocation validated that we, too, can lift our whole being—spirit, heart, body, mind, and will—to God. The steps she had to climb to attain this fullness were to practice trusting obedience in the will of the Father; to show chaste, respectful love for others in imitation of the Son; and to let her poverty of spirit be the portal to spreading word of God's reign. These three evangelical counsels honed her ability to listen to God's Word in her inner life, in her situation, in her relationships, and in her eventual service to the wider world. Suffering chiseled away with slow but steady strokes what was left of her resistance to becoming a living incarnation of deified love. In the end, her voided selfhood was turned by God into a holocaust of sacrificial love. Through her saintly death God deigned to release many signs of his Divine Mercy to a waiting world.

The blessings of spiritual childhood go beyond one or the other practice and become in due time second nature to seeking souls like Thérèse. The plan and purpose ordained by God for her cloistered life culminated in her choice to follow his lead in the most ordinary, utterly unspectacular situations. Her precarious physical condition left her with no pretensions other than to make this earth a portal to heaven.

Docility, self-abandoned love, and detachment were for Thérèse a formula for gathering the treasures daily life yielded like a profusion of garden flowers. With Teresa of Avila, she could say with certainty: "God alone suffices." It was her littleness that gave her the strength she needed to combat remnants of childishness embedded in her early character formation while excelling in the grace of spiritual childhood. Far from grieving over her imperfections, she took delight in the way God changed the obstacles associated with her hypersensitivity into occasions to grow in humility. She considered that the greatest favor God granted to her was the humiliating revelation of her nothingness and her incapacity for doing any good on her own. It never fails to surprise us that someone so ordinary could become such an extraordinary Doctor of the Church.

Second Facet of the New Evangelization

To appreciate the gift of every circumstance of daily life.

Questions for Reflection

1. Can you suggest three rules of life to enhance your own and others' sense of gratitude like, for example, stopping in its tracks the tendency to complain about anyone or anything?

2. Why is antipathy the enemy of evangelization? Can you offer an example of how ill will poisons the air of the teamwork and cooperation so necessary for any evangelizing task?

3. Can you detect remnants of childishness in your own character that may hamper your ability to serve others in a loving and mature Christian manner?

Closing Prayer

Lord, please fulfill my longing to go through life with a grateful heart as St. Thérèse always tried to do. Let me not wait for the perfect situation to witness to your truth but to do so in the exact circumstances in which I find myself. Help me to practice the ministry of the smile as the simplest way to overcome the impatience and judgmentalism that have no place in the New Evangelization. Amen.

3

The Little Way of Trust in Divine Mercy

Remember that as a child of light
I often forget to serve my King well.
Oh! Take pity on my great misery.
In your love, Jesus, forgive me.
"Jesus, My Beloved, Remember"[1]

Despite promises of reconciliation and forgiveness, we may still be tempted to see our faults as evils to be shunned rather than as pointers to instruct us in the life of the spirit. Infidelity is not a cause for discouragement but a call to live in the childlike trust that God sustains our smallest efforts with the greatest of graces. Reliance on Divine Mercy—not our own "do-it-yourself" mentality—is the key to lasting accomplishment. At times, we may fall short of our evangelical goals, but we ought not to consider ourselves a failure.

Thérèse observed that children learning to walk unavoidably fall down from time to time, and yet this awkwardness endears them to their parents and makes their first sure steps a cause for celebration. She also saw the connection between physical setbacks and spiritual progress. Life was for her not a problem to solve but a mystery to ponder. The drier she felt the more she observed that through bouts of *"exterior darkness*, [she] was inwardly illumined!"[2] Mortification of self-love enabled her to participate in Christ's own *kenosis* or self-emptying on the Cross. His thirst convinced her of the need to pray without ceasing for souls seeking God, who alone could fill their blessing cup to the full. Exactly because the Cross was too heavy for a child to carry, Christ bore its weight on his shoulders and initiated her climb upward to God: "The elevator which must raise me to heaven is Your arms, O Jesus! And for this I had no need to grow up, but rather I had to remain *little* and become this more and more."[3]

A shining facet of evangelical spirituality is to accept our littleness as the reason for our reliance on God. The vulnerability of her being led Thérèse to conclude that God would provide all she needed to fulfill Christ's commission to teach the nations from the confines of Carmel. The carefreeness of being like a little child enabled Thérèse to labor for God's glory whether or not her efforts were rewarded. Being a little ball with which God could play was enough reward for her. In desolation, when she probably felt like a lost child, helpless and alone, she clung to the truth of her friendship with a Playmate who promised never to desert her. She bypassed the ups and downs of her often volatile emotions and relied instead on Christ's promise not to leave her orphaned (cf. Jn 14:18). Had Thérèse not exercised the virtue of unshakeable confidence in the benevolence of God, she might not have been able to carry the physical, emotional, and spiritual crosses God gave her. On "down" days, when she walked in the garden amidst the beauty of roses in bloom and contemplated the bounty of God's first revelation in creation, she found consolation in prayer, saying:

I know, O my God, that you humble the proud soul but
to the one who humbles herself you give an eternity
of glory. So I want to put myself in the last rank and
to share your humiliations so as "to have a share with
you" in the kingdom of heaven.[4]

The virtue of childlike confidence permeated her soul to
such a degree that she believed lack of it offends Jesus and
opens us to the obstacles of discouragement and fear of
failure. What gives us confidence are not accomplishments
attained in life but the redemptive love of God. He comes
to our aid in proportion to our willingness to acknowledge our finitude. It is an ever-present reminder that long-
ings as infinite as ours for union with God can never be
satisfied in this limited life. Thérèse herself confesses that
the moment she heard that her sister Pauline had decided
to enter Carmel, "[She] shed bitter tears because [she] did
not yet understand the *joy* of sacrifice."[5]

Once she came to see the blessings of being a little
child, Thérèse understood that God "parcels out trials
only according to the strength He gives us."[6] Her confidence in God became one of the all-encompassing virtues
of her life. The selfless nature of her love enabled her to
mirror the excess of love that drew the Father to sacrifice
his Son for sinners like us. What motivated her to love others without expecting to receive love in return, was to do
as Jesus did. That is why she developed the disposition of
holy indifference in regard to the favors God may or may
not grant to his children. She served Jesus for his own sake
since he himself was her reward. Even when those around
her were benevolently oblivious to her charitable actions
and personal sacrifices, she behaved in the same way. An
often under-appreciated blessing of spiritual childhood

became for her the conviction that it is best to hide our sufferings from others and even, so to speak, from God, so as to remain cheerful givers. The dispensation of graces is up to God. It is up to us to accept with equanimity the trials and joys sent our way by our Beloved. In either case, they are invitations from God to test our good intentions and to reveal what we should do for others. Such facets of spiritual childhood spread from the Carmel of Lisieux to the farthest reaches of the globe.

Why was Jesus so fond of letting little children come to him? He paid them the highest compliment, saying that unless we become like them we cannot enter his kingdom (see Mk 10:15). Surely this privilege has nothing to do with the volatile demands of babyhood. It is not connected to bargaining nor to the expectation that if I do good works I deserve to receive divine graces. Such thoughts are detrimental to evangelization. What Thérèse exhibited were childlike qualities like trust and good humor, not childish petulance. She gave up the childishness of having to get her own way and chose instead to become spiritually mature.

Even a cursory reading of her autobiography reveals that her actions were edifying to others not because she performed them expertly but because she animated them with love. She tried to incorporate unnoticed sacrifices into the routines of daily obedience. She advanced in spiritual maturity not by virtue of self-imposed mortifications, which she was forbidden to perform anyway, but because she fulfilled with unfailing generosity and joy whatever was demanded of her. Her ministry was to be faithful to Christ in the midst of the most pedestrian activity.

It has been my privilege and humble honor to serve several cloistered Carmelites as a teacher of formative spirituality and as a retreat leader. I never fail to marvel at the rhythm of worship and work that characterizes their life in the convent. Surely Mary and Martha become one behind these walls. There is no activity that is more efficacious than another. One of the older nuns told me with a twinkle in her eyes, "I'm not able to cook anymore, but I can still do a bang-up job washing dishes and shining pans."

The lessons we learn from Thérèse's Carmelite life continue to mount. She deserves the accolade "apostle of the New Evangelization" because she understands the blessings of being a little child, like tending the sick and elderly without in the least needing to be lauded by one's community at home or in church. She accepted the truth that little children are often neither seen nor heard. That was fine with her. She delighted in small pleasures like a bunch of fresh flowers on her bedside table or special food on a feast day.

This same childlike spirit allowed her to look lovingly on the virtues her sisters displayed rather than to judge their faults. Fading into the background was the best assurance that communal merits would prevail. She felt that it was better to let the sisters keep their own opinions than to engage in gossip or in-fighting. It hurt her to think that they might conform to her point of view rather than trying to perceive God's will for them. She did her best to restore tranquility whenever trouble arose in the community. Her aim as God's emissary was to keep a cheerful countenance, even when the pain of breathing was almost more than she could bear. If others' misunderstanding made her suffer, she remained as silent as Jesus was before his accusers. When certain events did upset her, she learned how to redirect her attention to the Lord.

In this era of the New Evangelization, we have to expect that the vine-grower will put us through the process of pruning the dead branches of slavery to self in order to disengage us from whatever obstructs Christ-centered love. Thérèse probably imagined herself among the throngs of children waiting for a turn to sit on Jesus' lap. She felt the unbounded generosity of his love and wanted to do all she could to comfort him. Jesus saw in children the potential to grow in the perfection of charity. When little ones are truly loved they want so much to show their parents how much they appreciate their care. If evangelization were a mirror into which we could look, would we not see children walking hand in hand with mothers and fathers teaching them the faith? Might we not catch a glimpse of what unmitigated trust really means? Would we not want to dance with joy and play music on glad tambourines?

Third Facet of the New Evangelization

To live in the childlike trust that God bolsters our smallest efforts and that Divine Mercy is the key to lasting accomplishment despite the fact that we may fall short of our evangelical goals.

Questions for Reflection

1. Are you burdened by the heresy of perfectionism to such a degree that it hampers your evangelical efforts?

2. Can you accept with compassion your own and others' less than perfect behavior in family life, church, and society and learn to rely more on the mercy of God?

3. Why is the virtue of childlike confidence in Divine Mercy valued so highly by St. Thérèse? How does it lead to the perfection of charity?

Closing Prayer

Lord, in the face of the misunderstanding I am bound to encounter in the context of proclaiming your Word, calm my soul with frequent showings of your compassion. Bathe my misery in the cleansing waters of your mercy. When crosses seem too heavy to carry, let me relinquish them as would a child to your loving embrace and blessed benevolence. Amen.

4

The Little Way of Sacramental Life

O Jesus! on this day, you have fulfilled all my desires,
From now on, near the Eucharist, I shall be able
To sacrifice myself in silence, to wait for Heaven in peace.
Keeping myself open to the rays of the Divine Host,
In this furnace of love, I shall be consumed,
And like a seraphim, Lord, I shall love you.
"Canticle of a Soul. . . ."[1]

We do not know whether or not Thérèse had a premonition of an early death when she entered Carmel. What we do know is that by the time she passed through the portals of the cloister, she was already skilled in some of the secrets of spiritual living. For example, mortification "consisted in breaking my will, always so ready to impose itself on others, in holding back a reply, in rendering little services without recognition."[2] The practice of these *nothings* prepared her to be espoused to Jesus, but nothing was more important to Thérèse than the sacramental life.

The common ways of liturgy, Word, sacrament, and the devotional life are necessary supports of evangelization. Every time we receive the Eucharist, we experience communion with Jesus in our hearts and in the world he calls us to serve. In cooperation with the initiating and transforming grace of God, these ways become avenues to intimacy with the Trinity and daily recommitment to the Gospel. While contemplation of the saving mystery of Christ's humanity and divinity remains ineffable, the liturgy draws us as near to the Infinite as we finite worshippers can come. God's holy people are led to a fuller awareness of the faith through hearing and reading the Word in a variety of liturgical settings.

One setting I will never forget was a Zulu village in South Africa where Fr. Adrian and I, along with another Holy Ghost priest and colleague, were asked to speak to a group of newly catechized Christians after morning Mass. The celebrant was another missionary so the three of us were able to sit with the worshippers under the roof of their first consecrated chapel. It was built in the African style with a thatched roof and hand-carved benches. The voices of the gatherers rose in perfect harmony to adore the Lord. The offertory procession lasted for almost thirty minutes because people brought to the altar for a blessing samples of their crops, bouquets of freshly picked flowers, household items, and gift upon gift for their priests and teachers. I had tears in my eyes watching these believers receive the Eucharist with a reverence often missing in today's churches. These dear people reminded me never to take reception of Christ's Body and Blood for granted but to see every liturgy as an invitation to transformation.

Through the power of the Word, souls convert to Christ; hearts once hardened to belief are transformed; sinners repent, and ministry gains new meaning. Our tradition teaches that worthy reception of the sacraments leads us to Christian perfection. The Eucharist above all is the principal means of formation of the people of God; it is a fountain of grace and a powerful passageway to salvation. It is understood that the responsibility of every believer is to personalize in his or her devotional life these common ways of deepening faith. Such practices as praying the Rosary, venerating icons, making pilgrimages to sacred places, to mention only a few, become staging areas for personal encounters with the Good Shepherd, who comes to us in the silence of the night and the assignments of the day.

On April 9, 1888, the official day of Thérèse's entrance to the Carmelite cloister of Lisieux, her whole family joined her in the celebration of the liturgy and the reception of Holy Communion. However, her and their experiences were not the same:

> As soon as Jesus descended into the hearts of my relatives, I heard nothing around me but sobs. I was the only one who didn't shed any tears, but my heart was beating *so violently* it seemed impossible to walk when they signaled for me to come to the enclosure door. . . . Ah! What a moment that was! One would have to experience it to know what it is.[3]

Liturgy evangelizes us when we participate in it not as a routine event but as a mystery of wordless wonder that draws us closer to God; it is the fount from which all prayer and presence flows; it is the portal to Christian perfection. Although "it is not always possible in Carmel to practice the words of the Gospel according to the letter,"[4] Thérèse obligated herself to absorb and act upon each revelation of scripture in spirit and in truth. For example, when Jesus said in Matthew 5:42 "Give to everyone who begs from you, and do not refuse anyone who wants to borrow from you," she took this directive to mean that "one must not stay away from the Sisters who are always in the habit of asking for help. Neither should one be obliging in order to *appear* so or in the hope that another time the Sister whom one obliges will return the service. . . ."[5]

We ought to give up the habit of trying to predict where the Word will lead us and simply follow the path the Holy Spirit inspires. To give to others without expecting to receive anything in return was Thérèse's way of preserving serenity of heart: "It would satisfy self-love, for giving is a more generous act than lending, and then we make the Sister feel we don't depend on her services. Ah! how contrary are the teachings of Jesus to the feelings of our nature! Without the help of His grace it would be impossible not only to put them into practice but to even understand them."[6]

The question is: are we ready to let the sacraments of the Church transform our lives? In Thérèse's autobiography, we find detailed references to her Baptism, Confirmation, First Confession, and Communion and, at the end of her life, the Anointing of the Sick. After the grace she received at Christmas, she concluded: "Holy baptism must implant a very deep seed of the theological virtues [faith, hope, and charity] in souls since from childhood these virtues are already evident and since the hope of future goods suffices to have [us] accept sacrifices."[7] She viewed being baptized as her entrance to the paschal mystery and to a life of Trinitarian intimacy: ". . . for in one Spirit we were all baptized into one body" (1 Cor 12:13).

As was the custom in those days, shortly after her First Communion, she went on retreat to prepare for her Confirmation: "I was prepared with great care to receive the visit of the Holy Spirit, and I did not understand why greater attention was not paid to the reception of this sacrament of *Love*."[8] She awaited the Holy Spirit's visit with great happiness and she says: "I rejoiced at the thought of soon being a perfect Christian and especially at that of having eternally on my forehead the mysterious cross the Bishop marks when conferring this sacrament."[9] Without it, she did not think that she would have had the strength to be a missionary in service of every soul in the world.

Thérèse tells us that she could never understand why approaching the sacrament of Penance caused certain hearts to flutter anxiously. Even her first confession is "a sweet memory for me!"[10] To tell the priest her sins, to receive absolution, and to go forth with greater devotion were numbered among her greatest blessings. Once when she had to go to the infirmary because she was coughing violently, she was given the opportunity of making a general confession. It left great peace in her soul, for "God did not permit the slightest cloud to come and trouble me."[11]

On another occasion she felt an unforgettable consolation when she heard her confessor declare that she had never committed a mortal sin. "Then he [Fr. Pichon] added, 'Thank God for what He has done for you; had He abandoned you, instead of being a little angel, you would have become a little demon.'"[12] It was easy for her to believe that this would have been her fate: "I felt how weak and imperfect I was and gratitude flooded my soul."[13]

Even a writer as prolific and as talented as Thérèse had trouble finding the words to describe her unspeakable joy when partaking of Christ's Body and Blood in the sacrament of the Eucharist. She remembers every detail of the day she received her First Holy Communion. That was when Jesus himself gave her the kiss of love and when she promised to love him forever. It was an experience of fusion. Jesus and Thérèse were no longer two but one. It was as if she "had vanished as a drop of water is lost in the immensity of the ocean."[14] Bold as this request may seem in so young a soul, Thérèse asked Jesus to do her a favor: to take away her *liberty*. Feeble and fragile as she was, freedom of will frightened her. She wanted to be united body and soul to the Divine Strength, so much so that tears of consolation covered her cheeks. The onlookers thought she was sad, but she was happier than she had ever been.

Thérèse's intuition that Communion would be an eternal event in heaven was confirmed when she received the sacrament of Anointing. Now the veil of this sweet encounter would be torn through and, as St. John of the Cross said, she would be dying of love. Her anointing took place on July 30. That evening she received Viaticum.[15] For a while, the coughing up of blood ceased and, starting on August 5, she was granted a short period of relief; then a new attack began on August 15. A few days later, on August 19, she received Communion for the last time and on September 30, after an agony of two days, she left her body and met her Beloved.

When Thérèse returns in memory to the ten years she spent in the convent, she recalls, in addition to the sacramental life, the importance of her daily devotions—praying the Rosary, venerating the saints, celebrating holy days like May crownings and professions, following the Stations of the Cross, fastings and feastings. As was her custom, she saw in every "little nothing" an opportunity for adoration and a call to Christian action. Routines some other members of the community may have seen as pointless and boring assumed for her a radiance beyond all telling. Such attention to detail made it impossible for her to take anything for granted. She saw the Eucharist in everything. This practice in itself made her less agitated and more patient. It prevented her from becoming joyless and judgmental. She began to see everywhere the sacredness Jesus saw when he blessed and broke the bread. After the Resurrection (see Lk 24:30), he was recognized in this seemingly inconspicuous act.

In the solitude of Carmel, God announced the silent splendor of the everyday, the shared treasure of the ordinary. One day when Thérèse was going to Communion, she felt as if the Lord was not yet satisfied with her. So she said to herself, ". . . if I receive only half a host today, this will cause me great sorrow, and I shall believe that Jesus comes regretfully into my heart."[16] Here's how this ordinary experience of compunction became extraordinary: "I approached [the altar], and oh, what joy! For the first time in my life I saw the priest take two hosts which were well separated from each other and place them on my tongue! You can understand my joy and the sweet tears of consolation I shed when beholding a mercy so great!"[17]

In each of her sisters, Thérèse saw what all of us have in common. At the base of her evangelizing dispositions was this shared longing for oneness in the Lord. Her life, like ours, became an ebb and flow between receiving inspirations from the Holy Spirit and incarnating them in daily life. Loving the ordinary and seeing Jesus in it prevents us from boasting about anything or from calling attention to ourselves. The more we live in love, the more each moment becomes a manifestation of the mystery. When that is our aim, our old ways of dictating to

God vanish and we submit in prayerful surrender to his will. He makes us broken bread and poured-out wine. Our whole being becomes the place where God's glory abides (see Ps 26:8).

Invited to speak at a prestigious Catholic college for women, I was not surprised when the sister hosting me asked if I would like to meet the "treasure" of their community. For some reason, I thought she said the "treasurer" so I was taken aback when, instead of heading for the administrative offices, she directed me to the infirmary. When we got off the elevator on the fourth floor of the motherhouse, we walked together down a long, sparkling clean corridor to the last room and opened the door. In her hospital bed lay an elderly nun so fragile one could almost see the skeleton behind her skin but so radiant with joy that an ethereal light shone through her whole being.

"Here," sister said, "is the treasure of our community." Her smile revealed why. She greeted me warmly, said she had heard my presentation on the audio system connected to her room, and blessed me with the news that she had been praying for me from the moment I arrived on campus. What I learned was that in this active, apostolically-minded congregation, she was the contemplative who fueled the fire of love that enabled their work to continue. She witnessed to the paschal mystery, to the dying and rising of Jesus, that had a central place in Thérèse's heart, too: "Do you not know that all of us who have been baptized into Christ Jesus were baptized into his death? Therefore we have been buried with him by baptism into death, so that, just as Christ was raised from the dead by the glory of the Father, so we too might walk in newness of life" (Rom 6:3–4).

Lamentable as her premature death was for her sisters, Thérèse had been prepared for it by the Lord. He would keep her here for as long as he needed her. Living to give him glory was all she desired. Dying was the prelude to rising with him so that the work begun in her in time would continue for eternity. She began her evangelizing efforts at the foot of the Cross. It was for her the summit of faith, hope, and charity.

Participation in the paschal mystery is inseparable from cooperation with God's grace. The slightest nod from Jesus was enough to make Thérèse give up everything and follow him. Going forth did not mean performing great deeds but surrendering in gratitude to what lay before her. Did not Jesus do the same by surrendering his will to the Father's and dispensing forgiving love through his death on the Cross? Always what is impossible for us is possible for God:

> You know better than I do my weakness and imperfection; you know very well that never would I be able to love my Sisters as You love them, unless *You*, O my Jesus, *loved them in me*. It is because You wanted to give me this grace that You made Your *new* commandment. Oh! How I love this new commandment since it gives me the assurance that Your Will is *to love in me* all those you command me to love![18]

Even after her death, Thérèse had the sense that God would send her forth to do his will. She would not sit sedately around the heavenly throne; rather she would roll up her sleeves and get to work. And so, on July 17, 1897, a few weeks before her release to eternal life, she made what has come to be known as her most sublime prediction:

I feel that my mission is about to begin, my mission of making others love God as I love Him, my mission of teaching my little way to souls. If God answers my requests, my heaven will be spent on earth until the end of the world. Yes, I want to spend my heaven doing good on earth.[19]

Fourth Facet of the New Evangelization

To make worthy reception of the sacraments, especially the Eucharist, the epicenter of our evangelical life, and to carry its efficacy into everyday reality.

Questions for Reflection

1. Why must there be in any and all facets of the New Evangelization a reverent reliance on the sacraments, especially those of Baptism, Reconciliation, Confirmation, and Holy Communion?

2. Have you paid enough attention to the loving relationship of intimacy and transformation conferred upon you with every worthy reception of the Body and Blood of Christ in eucharistic adoration?

3. Do you see, as Thérèse did, the indelible bridge between sacramental reverence and a fuller living of the dying and rising of Jesus?

Closing Prayer

Lord, increase my love of liturgy, Word, and sacrament that I may share this love with others both with and without words. Raise my heart and mind to the mystery of wordless wonder that draws me closer to you in every eucharistic celebration. From the joy of Baptism to the sick-bed of anointed suffering, let me benefit from the efficacy of the sacramental system established by you and continually brought to fruition in your evangelizing Church. Amen.

5

The Little Way of Abandonment to Divine Providence

Jesus will weave your crown
If you only desire His love,
If your heart abandons itself in Him,
He will have you reign forever.
"The Queen of Heaven to Her Beloved Child. . . ."[1]

The fifth step to in-depth evangelization suggests that our duty is not to concentrate only on this or that mission but to see the whole of life as one entire mission of surrender to the will of God. So far we have focused on the efficacy of hiddenness, the richness of the ordinary, and the blessings of being a little child. Now Thérèse inspires us to pursue an outlook contrary to our expectations. In a world that prides itself on independence and self-sufficiency, she instills in us evangelizers the truth that our primary starting point must be a spirit of self-abnegation, which is to say the annihilation of anything in us resistant to humble obedience to the Father's will.

One of the Little Sisters of the Poor, who became Fr. Adrian's in-residence caregiver for the final two years of his life, became a true "soul-friend" to both of us. She studied our books, listened to our tapes, and came to live one of the main tenets of Father's teaching: to trust God's plan for our lives and to believe that it will outshine our fondest expectations, however contrary it may be to them.

Sister had ministered for years in Australia, among the Aboriginal people, and would have liked to live with them for the rest of her life, but a serious auto accident made it necessary for her to return to the United States and eventually be missioned in Pittsburgh. She accepted this "curve ball" with grace and gratitude. Had it not happened she would not have met Fr. Adrian, benefitted from his "ministry of presence," and found a way to continue her study of the topic she loved most: in-depth spiritual formation. Despite her own aches and pains, she rejoiced that she could join her whole being to Christ on the Cross and offer her suffering for every needy member of his Mystical Body.

To appreciate this spirit, we have to look no further than the scripture account of Jesus' agony in the Garden of Gethsemane (see Mt 26:36–42). He knew that his hour had come. To drink this cup was his destiny as Son of God and Son of Man. Despite his human resistance to the debilitating suffering he foresaw, he offered his total *yes* to the Father. This example of the abandoned heart of Jesus would not have been forgotten by Thérèse during the agony of her incurable illness. Consumption claimed her body but paradoxically its infliction released her soul to such a degree that even on her death bed she was an exemplary evangelizer. Everyone around her was edified by her peace, her gentleness, her serenity, and her unfailing humor. This growth in Christian virtue would have been inconceivable had she not been converted already to the need for appreciative abandonment to the love-will of Father, Son, and Holy Spirit. She knew from experience that suffering, about which we can do nothing, is an invitation to union with our crucified Lord.

Abandonment disposes us to evangelization because it modifies our expectations of outcomes that appear to be successful in our eyes. Many dedicated ministers of the Gospel burn out because so few people come to their meticulously planned meetings; because donations level off or go down; because the number of worshippers stays more or less the same despite the new plans "guaranteed" to boost Church growth.

Abandonment to God's will caused Thérèse to turn toward him and away from her habit of having to be her father's little queen. It reduced her need to be coddled by her older sisters or to aspire to rush off to far away missionary outposts to serve Jesus. *The more she abandoned herself to living her life as one act of love, the more she brought together sanctity and service, contemplation and action.* Behind plain appearances she saw people thirsting for Christ as much as he thirsted for them just as they were, without any frills.

Thérèse enjoyed the peace of Jesus by accepting, as he did, that nothing happens outside of God's loving and allowing will. *Conformity to Christ was not an exercise in passivity but an act of receptivity that bore lasting fruit.* She abandoned herself to the reality that she would not live to a ripe old age the moment she began to cough up blood. That was the way it had to be. It would be useless to dwell on end stage issues when there was so much to accomplish each day. There was no better homily anyone could preach than to see such an abandoned evangelizer at work. Thérèse experienced that "God gives the hundredfold in this life to those souls who leave everything for love of Him."[2] In the light of such exquisite expressions of his mercy, she could conclude without hesitation: "Neither do I desire any longer suffering or death, and still I love them both; it is love alone that attracts me, however. . . . Now, abandonment alone guides me. I have no other compass! I can no longer ask for anything with fervor except the accomplishment of God's will in my soul without any creature being able to set obstacles in the way."[3]

Thérèse's evangelical zeal came from her knowledge that God would accomplish in her what she could never do on her own. That is why, toward the end of her autobiography, she wrote words every evangelizer ought to commit to memory: ". . . charity consists in bearing with the faults of others, in not being surprised at their weaknesses, in being edified by the smallest acts of virtue we see them practice . . . it is no longer a question of loving one's neighbor as oneself but of loving him as He, Jesus, has loved him, and will love him to the consummation of the ages."[4]

Abandonment to Divine Providence leads us to the perfection of love. On the day of her profession (September 8, 1890), Thérèse carried on her heart a letter in which she wrote to her Spouse: "Jesus, I ask You for nothing but peace, and also love, infinite love without any limits other than Yourself; love which is no longer I but You, my Jesus."[5] Like a dying swan, her song to him became more and more melodious the closer she came to breathing her last breath. To both her sisters and her confessor, she said a few months before she passed away: "*I am not dying; I am entering into life!*"[6] Abundant love pervaded her abandoned heart to such a degree that it cast out her fear (see 1 Jn 4:18). She viewed her passing from this life as a passage to the permanent embrace Jesus had earned for her on the Cross.

Knowing this truth was the only way I could have endured my mother's death from Alzheimer's disease on December 21, 1998. The loss of one's parent is traumatic enough, but I had also been asked by God to yield to him my best friend. For months before her passing, I had begged the Lord to let me be with her at that moment. This was a request he heard and honored because I made it home from a wintry out-of-town engagement. I rushed to her bedside at the care center where she lived during the final stripping this disease demands. Thank God, she was not alone but under the continuous watch of skilled and compassionate caregivers, who showed me daily what Christ would do in this situation.

I visited Mother almost every day during the last years of her life. We walked and talked and prayed together, looked at photo albums, and listened to music, though she no longer knew who I was. As she was fading from life, I imagined her falling into the arms of Jesus as she passed from the radical diminishment of Alzheimer's to the radiant release planned for her by God since the beginning of her life. The earthly window closed; the heavenly portals opened at three o'clock in the morning. She would spend her Christmas in eternity.

Living the paschal mystery of Christ's dying and rising stripped Thérèse, as it must strip us, of childish illusions that veil the virtues of evangelization. From being an immature fledgling full of faults, Thérèse became a mature woman fearlessly committed to giving her all for God. In

the midst of her trial of faith, in the throes of interior suffering, she found what the true meaning of prayer was.
It became for her "an aspiration of the heart . . . a simple
glance directed to heaven . . . a cry of gratitude and love in
the midst of trial as well as joy."[7]

Fifth Facet of the New Evangelization

To abandon all that we are and do, and all of its outcomes, to the abandoned heart of Jesus and to let his *yes*
to the Father become the guiding light of our mission and
ministry.

Questions for Reflection

1. In this action-oriented, do-it-yourself world, how
   would you identify with the abandoned heart of Jesus
   whose only food was "to do the will of him who sent
   me and to complete his work" (Jn 4:34)?

2. What does this sentence mean to you: *"Conformity to
   Christ was not an exercise in passivity but an act of receptivity that bore lasting fruit"*?

3. In what way does abandonment to Divine Providence
   strengthen virtues like evangelical zeal and the perfection of love?

Closing Prayer

Lord, help me not to get so caught up in the details of
my evangelical plans and projects that I lose the overall
vision and mission of surrender to the Father's will. Mod-
ify my expectations of what success means in the eyes of

the world and teach me, even at times of apparent failure, to be more faithful. Under the inspiration of St. Thérèse, let my life become one act of love devoted to sanctity and service. Amen.

6

The Little Way of Experiencing Friendship with God and Others

Set free from the world
And without any support,
Your grace overwhelms me,
My only friend!
"The Atom of the Sacred Heart"[1]

Being a loner is an unworkable formula for successful evangelization. It leads to a narrowing of vision that can make us either too fanatical or too forgetful of what being called, committed, consecrated, and commissioned really entails. Even Jesus himself needed those he called friends (see Jn 15:15) to carry his teaching to Jews and Gentiles alike. He could count on them to follow him when fainter hearts turned away.

Evangelization unfolds to the fullest degree when we come together—in friendship, in partnership, in companionship. Team work expands our creativity and boosts our stamina. When we share insights into what needs to be done, we notice that the demands made upon us by Jesus are less heavy to bear.

Ever since the cofounding of the Epiphany Association on May 4, 1979, we have been aware that the model we follow and rely upon is not that of a management team but of a gathering of friends. This friendship extends to board members, benefactors, and the students we serve. It allows for the gift of agreeing to disagree agreeably! We withhold the barbs of competition and seek those areas where we can come together in spiritual communion with Christ at the center. We sense the "all for one, one for all" mentality taught to us by Fr. Adrian since his war experiences in the Netherlands. For him, the greatest example of betrayal occurred when people he thought he could trust to deliver the food he and other members of the Dutch underground had painstakingly gathered kept it for themselves. They failed not only their fellow sufferers, they betrayed one of the main lessons the Gospel they purported to follow teaches: to lay down their life for their friends (see Jn 15:13).

The friendship facet of evangelization ties in with the Teresian tradition that prayer is intimate conversation with the One who loves us. It must precede and accompany all that we do. Prayer promotes nearness to God and leads to a sense of communion with others. Friendly eyes and a warm smile inspire belief in the Good News. People listened to the groundbreaking instructions of Jesus not only because they respected his rabbinic wisdom but also because he told story after story to aid their understanding of what his mission of mercy really meant. He used the art of friendly persuasion to convince them to become "a new creation [in] everything" (Gal 6:15).

Whether or not Thérèse realized what an amazing storyteller she was, her honesty is irresistible, her wisdom as timeless as it is timely. She tells of her dependency on family members and the friends with whom she corresponded. (See the Appendix of this book, "Thérèse in Her Own Words").

Moving back and forth from poetry to prose, her teachings delight us intellectually and spiritually because of the friendly, down-to-earth way she presents them. Though she had little formal schooling, Thérèse listened to the Lord as one would to a good friend; she heard him speaking to her in scripture and in the writings of her favorite spiritual masters. She teaches us that we can neither be friends of Jesus nor be befriended by him unless we practice such virtues as simplicity, humility, and cheerfulness.

We never find Thérèse standing on a pedestal, preaching to us; rather she shares with us, as if we were among her best friends, her experience that the limits of life contain an encyclopedia of blessings. She never doubts that Jesus conveys to us the "words of eternal life" (Jn 6:68). We must both conserve and disseminate them by our evangelizing efforts, however noticed or unnoticed they may be.

Although Thérèse's personal charm could be persuasive, she deferred any compliments she received to Jesus. Amidst her dark nights of suffering in sense and spirit, many thought of her as the clown of the community. Once God deigned to imprint his divine stamp on her heart, her joy was to be found in drawing souls to him. Her encounters with Christ enhanced her natural gifts and allowed her to use these evangelical endowments for a higher purpose.

Once Thérèse bound herself to Jesus as his friend forever, she came to the candid conclusion that the best mortification she could practice consisted in breaking her will which is "always so ready to impose itself on others, in holding back a reply, in rendering little services without any recognition. . . ."[2] She never wanted anyone to imitate her; her happiness consisted in their coming to know Jesus more. It was his face she wanted them to see. Behind external gestures of friendliness like a smile instead of a frown, she hoped that those she touched would internalize the joy of the Gospel, leading them to deny themselves, take up their cross, and follow Jesus (see Lk 14:27).

Initial conversion is to be followed by a second conversion that opens one's human spirit wholly to the directing power of the Holy Spirit. It heals the split between belief outwardly professed and faith inwardly lived. The friendship between Thérèse and Jesus was that perfect blend of contemplation and action modeled so beautifully by his encounter with Mary and Martha (see Lk 10:38–42).

The radical nature of her desire to be Jesus' friend led this future saint to repent any time she got in the way of what God wanted to do through her. Though her fondness for consolations did not cease, though she admitted that at times she still displayed certain attachments, she named "spiritual aridity [as her] daily bread and, deprived of all consolation, she was still the happiest of creatures since all her desires had been satisfied."[3]

This detachment from any "lesser god" ultimately prepared Thérèse for that fateful moment when total darkness would descend upon her. It happened on Easter Day, 1896. Three days before that, on Holy Thursday, she had begun to vomit blood. Immediately she interpreted this event as a call from her Divine Spouse. What she could not have foreseen was the trial that God would inflict on her during the last eighteen months of her life, a trial that threatened to crack her faith and erode their friendship. It was during this time that she asked the sisters to remove from her room certain medications that might tempt her to take an overdose and put a premature end to God's perfect timing over life and death.

The mist that had surrounded her off and on for several months became thicker; it penetrated into her soul and enveloped her so much that it was no longer possible for her to find the sweet image of her heavenly homeland. Everything worthwhile disappeared. No matter how much dryness she may have experienced previously, her faith had kept her in touch with the heavenly encounter awaiting her. Now even that image was obscured in a cloud of unknowing so dense that no image, no perception, no concept of God was left for her perusal.

All the comforting remembrances of childhood, like that of playing with the boy Jesus in Nazareth, disappeared. The dark night of the spirit, with the testing of faith that accompanies it, inflicted itself upon her until her last breath. Only in the final hours before she passed into heaven was she lifted up in a blissful ebb and flow to the homeland she longed to inhabit. Yet this ethereal seeing was short-lived. More often than not, she lost the link between God's presence and her current cross due to the thickness of the darkness that engulfed her.

That is why it is all the more remarkable that on March 9, 1897, she had great fun relating to a priest with whom she was corresponding an incident about the cook at the convent who had trouble preparing a lobster. The creature leapt out of the pot of boiling water, convincing the cook that it must be possessed by the devil! This hilarious episode greatly amused the nuns at recreation. At the very moment when she showed such gaiety she was gravely ill. She had difficulty swallowing her food. Every day she ran a temperature. The treatment at that time consisted mainly of painful cauterizations. In the epicenter of this tortuous episode, she made others feel happy. They should enjoy their life. These trials were hers, not theirs.

Thérèse saw such sufferings as an integral part of what God had willed for her good. They did not diminish her love of life nor dampen the encouragement she gave everyone around her. Frail as her humanity was, her transfiguration in Christ gained in strength. So deep was their friendship that she could now go beyond the limits of earthly life and be Christ for others. She knew that the light of the Divine could not filter through her heart into theirs if she allowed its chambers to be clogged by a plethora of disquieting considerations. If the motivation out of which she acted was not that of selfless surrender, her actions risked being unresponsive to God's will. No amount of turmoil on the surface of life was able to disturb her inmost center: ". . . for I assure you there is *no exaggeration* in my *little soul*. Within it all is calm and at rest."[4]

The spiritual resignation displayed by Thérèse in her final hours reveals how vigilant she was about guarding her heart. She kept telling herself that Jesus thirsts for love because, even among his disciples, he found few hearts "who [surrendered] to Him without reservations."[5]

To understand the true meaning of Christ's love for us, we, too, must die hour by hour to ourselves. Nothing ought to pain us more than evidence of our own egoism. Death to self-centeredness has to be our ultimate goal as the new evangelizers. Just as St. John of the Cross taught Thérèse the efficacy of resignation and solitude, so she teaches us what we need to do to free ourselves from the traps of our self-centeredness and become more like Jesus in the Father's eyes.

Fr. Adrian shared many memories of the soul-friend he knew for the first several years of his religious life. He was a wonderful young man named Marinus ("Rinus") Scholtes. Both of them were born in The Hague and returned there for summer holidays. In the training they received for the priesthood, starting with the junior seminary, they found through prayer and companionship ways to fulfill their longing to be of one heart and mind in the Lord.

Rinus was as good at sports as Adrian was at study, but their differences paled in comparison to their mutual commitment to be and become other Christ's. Like Thérèse, Rinus died of tuberculosis at the age of twenty-two, shortly before he was to take final vows. Death could not end his and Adrian's friendship. In fact, Rinus promised Adrian that he would devote his heaven to guarding their goals of spiritual formation on earth. It was to Rinus's prayers that Fr. Adrian often attributed his own survival and the fulfillment of his mission in the Epiphany Association.

All of us together constitute a community of sinners on the way to becoming a communion of saints. Over the course of time, such refashioning made Thérèse more compassionate and tolerant toward the fallibility of the human condition. As a corollary to the virtue of patience, she knew when to be silent for the love of God. The mortifying process sheds light on what death to the egocentric aspects of our being really means. We efface ourselves in deference to others' needs. We let them become Christ for us, knowing that "He is always using His creatures as instruments to carry on His work in souls."[6]

Thérèse was content to be the little brush Jesus had selected to paint his own image in all those entrusted to her care, especially the novices. Her Friend enabled her to listen to his voice in whatever situation she found herself. However severe the trials she would have to undergo, she knew she could turn to the Lord of glory alive in the center of her soul. Jesus was her citadel of strength and her calm pool of serenity. Just as Thérèse gave herself to him so, too, must we. Jesus keeps his promise. He raises our inglorious frame to the light of his glory until, in truth, our life becomes one act of love.

Sixth Facet of the New Evangelization

To be a friend of Jesus and to extend this gift of faithful friendship to all those entrusted to our care in family life, Church, and society.

Questions for Reflection

1. Do you agree that evangelization is intrinsically relational, that the Gospel is more caught than taught, that Jesus had good reasons for calling us friends (see Jn 15:15)?

2. Can you describe a personal encounter with Christ that both enhanced your sense of being called by him and of being directed to modes of discipleship in keeping with your gifts and talents?

3. Has your desire to be a friend of Jesus led to a renewed commitment to befriend others for his sake?

Closing Prayer

Lord, thank you for being the most faithful friend I know and for widening the circle of friendship that preserves and expands my faith, for to pray together is to stay together. Let every fiber of my life radiate the joy of the Gospel. Let the Christ in me meet and greet the Christ in all those whose feet I am to wash (see Jn 13:5). Lead me to new levels of intimacy with the Trinity. So transform me that affliction serves to advance my flight to you in bonds of friendship lasting from time to eternity. Amen.

7

The Little Way of Renunciation

Flame of Love, consume me unceasingly.
Life of an instant, your burden is so heavy to me!
Divine Jesus, make my dream come true:
To die of Love!
"Living on Love"[1]

In prose, poetry, and prayer, Thérèse celebrates the mystery of the Cross, which, as she once wrote to her sister Celine, is love pushed to the point of heroism. There could be no greater example of self-emptying love than that poured forth by our crucified and risen Lord. Only by following in the footsteps of Jesus could she turn limiting experiences of loss, suffering, and death into life-giving blessings. That is why the breaking points in her own life, as when her "second mother," Pauline entered Carmel, became breakthroughs to paths of sanctity hitherto unknown and unexplored.

In a world as bound to analytical logic as our own, the Cross can be a stumbling block to evangelism. We either accept it or we don't. We either mock the mystery or bend our knee in obedience to the Father's loving and allowing will. Frail as she was, Thérèse found the courage to fulfill her call to mirror Christ's gracious gift of redemption.

In an oft-cited exchange—representing a kind of cat-
echesis between Thérèse and her sister Celine—the meaning of God's grace became clear. When as a child this
mystery of Divine Mercy puzzled her, Celine sent Thérèse
into the sewing room to fetch a thimble and into the
kitchen to find a tumbler. Then she told her to fill both
vessels to the brim with water and inform her which one
was most full. Thérèse replied that both vessels were filled
to their capacity. And so, said Celine, that is how it is with
God's grace. One soul might be a thimble, another a tumbler, but both are filled to the fullest extent of their potential to become holy.

Once she entered Carmel, Thérèse seemed to be graced
with an ever maturing ability to show a similar love for
everyone she encountered, from eager novices to irri-
table elders. Maybe she concluded that the community
was like a hospital full of sick souls who needed excellent
doctors like Thérèse to heal them. What the Cross might
have lacked in worldly power, it made up for in supernatural love. Jesus loved his foes as well as his friends.
He sought to change their hearts and to reveal truths that
would give them new motives for behaving benevolently.
Like Thérèse, we, too, need to concentrate less on questions that have no answers (why would one so brilliant
have to die so young?) and more on living the mystery of
the Cross.

For the two and a half years that our Epiphany Academy faculty, headed by myself and Fr. Adrian, taught a
four-day course in "Spiritual Formation and Pastoral
Care" for the chaplains of the United States Navy, we met
many wonderful men and women representing at that
time (1987–1989) eighty-six different faith groupings.

One Catholic chaplain, with whom we became friends, related to us an amazing story of renunciation. Finding himself on deployment at a new naval base, he strove to excel in every duty, coming to his office earlier than necessary and departing at a late hour—all to impress his commanding officer, a Lutheran layman. One morning, after he had been there for about three months, the commander knocked on his office door and asked him if he could spare a moment. Father saluted sharply and invited him to take a seat. Then, as he told us, the commander paused for a moment before asking him the last question he could have expected. It was, "Where do you fathers go when you fathers need to remember who you fathers are?" He was dumbfounded, but he replied, "I guess we go on retreat." Then the commander gave him three days off to do just that. He called a center nearby, made his reservations, and returned to his quarters to pack. In one duffel bag, he put his personal items, a bible, and his breviary. In the other, he stuffed a bunch of paperwork he still had to do and some books he wanted to read when he had the time. Then he drove to the retreat house.

When he got there, he opened the trunk of his car and stood looking at the two duffel bags—the one with his overnight gear and the one with his "work to do." He said it was as if a force of some sort flowed down his arm and compelled him to slam the trunk on the working bag. It took him the first two of the three days to quiet himself inwardly and rethink his calling, bible and breviary in hand. He knew when he returned to base that he had to renounce his one-sided career track of being a military chaplain and return to his true vocation of being a chaplain who happened to be in the military. When his commander

stopped in to "debrief" the retreat and heard his obser-
vations, he smiled and said to Father, "Thank you. I have
many officers working on my staff, but what I really need
is a man of God. Could we say a little prayer of thanks
together?"

One fruit of evangelization is to commend to prayer
what we can neither grasp nor change. We do not question
God's ways, for they are not ours. It is enough to know that
God gives us the strength we need to accept what comes
and to profit from it. Not to conform to God's will was for
Thérèse both an abuse of our freedom and a frightening
descent into disobedience. One day she received the kiss
of Jesus and, from that point on, she was able to conclude:
"Had not Thérèse asked Him to take away her *liberty*, for
her *liberty* frightened her? She felt so feeble and fragile that
she wanted to be united forever to the divine Strength!"[2]

Evangelizing amidst the ordinary routines of life with
hope and patience as well as with realistic expectations of
success, can be a difficult burden to bear. It teaches us that
we must operate as part of, never apart from, God's plan,
mysterious as it may be. As long as we do not lose sight of
the enduring mercy of God, we may be shown by means
of grace that no obstacle is so great we cannot overcome it.

Despite the tragic interludes that accompany evangelization, consolations may come when we least expect them.
I myself recall a lonely summer night, walking under the
stars and there, in my own backyard, feeling uplifted by
their beauty. Though the day had been filled with a lit-
any of little crosses (a friend hospitalized, an expected call
that never came through, an overdue bill I thought had
been paid), these shining stars seemed to put it in perspective. This gifted moment reminded me of what passes and

of what lasts forever. The mystery of transforming love encompassed the cross of my sadness and brought welcome relief. Reminders of the disappointments everyday life holds can be discouraging, but living the paschal mystery gives us a new perspective.

One danger Thérèse faced in the cloister was the temptation to turn "molehills" into "mountains." Gossip erodes Gospel values unless one is willing to redirect one's thoughts to a more transcendent plane of meaning. The less attention one pays to inconveniences and disappointments, the more one begins to access the "bigger picture." This look leads to the kind of shift in consciousness Thérèse describes here:

> For a long time at evening meditation, I was placed in front of a Sister who had a strange habit and I think many lights because she rarely used a book during meditation. This is what I noticed: as soon as this Sister arrived, she began making a strange little noise which resembled the noise one would make when rubbing two shells, one against the other. I was the only one to notice it because I had extremely sensitive hearing (too much so at times). Mother, it would be impossible for me to tell you how much this little noise wearied me. I had a great desire to turn my head and stare at the culprit who was very certainly unaware of her "click." This would be the only way of enlightening her. However, in the bottom of my heart I felt it was much better to suffer this out of love for God and not to cause the Sister any pain. I remained calm, therefore, and tried to unite myself to God and to forget the little noise. Everything was useless. I felt the perspiration inundate me, and I was obliged simply to make a prayer of suffering; however, while suffering, I searched for a way of doing it without annoyance and with peace and joy, at least

in the interior of my soul. I tried to love the little noise
which was so displeasing; instead of trying not to hear
it (impossible), I paid close attention so as to hear it well,
as though it were a delightful concert, and my prayer
(which was not the *Prayer of Quiet*) was spent in offering
this concert to Jesus.[3]

Thérèse's capacity to turn the tables on judgmentalism
enabled her to obey Christ's caution to judge not so that
we will not be judged (see Lk 6:37). Her moment-by-mo-
ment yes to the Father, in ways unnoticed by others but
known full well to God, helped her to grow in humility
and self-abnegation. She was able to remain an evangelizing force under intense trials of faith because she had by
now trained herself to see them as life-giving. They were
both crosses God asked her to carry and crossroads to a
holier life. The seed of suffering fell on fertile ground in
Thérèse's soul; no amount of pain could defeat her faith in
the power of redemption. She found confirmation of the
"little way" in the sacred words she welcomed daily into
her heart. She says that "in them I find what is necessary
for my poor soul, I am constantly discovering in them new
lights, hidden and mysterious meanings."[4] Such formative reading of holy scripture enabled her to excel in her
evangelizing role in the Church. Thérèse teaches us how
to be instruments of God's will in this world, united so
intimately to Jesus that he lives and acts in us. This plung-
ing of our soul into the furnace of Divine Love resembles
the "surrender of the little child who sleeps without fear
in its Father's arms."[5]

The Carmelite lesson learned from St. John of the
Cross—that renunciation is the only way to liberation—
had a profound effect on Thérèse. Every sacrifice she

made, every task she performed, would be pleasing to Jesus as long as she forgot herself and allowed his crucified love to be reflected in her whole being. Only then could affliction advance her flight to God. The same struggle is felt by every evangelizing heart. Suffering in some form accompanies us the moment we move from self-enclosed isolation to world-embracing love. The best way to win the battle is to take the least complicated path: "Instead of going and hiding away in a corner, to weep over its misery and to die of sorrow, the little bird turns towards its beloved sun. . . ."[6]

Thérèse would never have wanted to suffer for suffering's sake. She chose freely to conform to Christ crucified and explains what she means by sharing an insight that came to her after reception of the Eucharist: "Up until this time, I had suffered without *loving* suffering, but since this day I felt a real love for it. I also felt the desire of loving only God, of finding my joy only in Him."[7] On her own she was too weak to perform any feat other than that of releasing innumerable graces through acts of unconditional love.

Suffering interpreted through the lens of the Cross raised Thérèse to new levels of self-understanding and enabled her to console others in empathy with their afflictions. Her example of the crossover between time and eternity proved that we humans are like amphibious creatures: one foot of ours is on the shore of the finite, and the other is in the sea of the Infinite. Living the paschal mystery lets us see meaning in apparent meaninglessness. With the Apostle Paul we can boast of our affliction because "[it] produces endurance, and endurance produces character, and character produces hope, and hope does not disappoint us, because God's love has been poured into our hearts through the Holy Spirit that has been given to us" (Rom 5:3–5).

If we doubt the veracity of this evangelical witness, we can glance in a looking glass, as Thérèse might have done, and say to ourselves: "Nothing I have to endure—no pain, insult, or injury—can be as devastating as what Jesus took upon himself from my sake." Instead of trying to dissuade ourselves from fulfilling our Christian commission, might it not be wiser to say with Thérèse: "I am but a poor little thing who would return to nothingness if Your divine grace did not give me life from one moment to the next."[8]

Seventh Facet of the New Evangelization

To enter as fully as possible into the mystery of the Cross, knowing that the victory belongs to Jesus, whose commission to go and teach the nations requires that we embrace his dying and celebrate his rising.

Questions for Reflection

1. What do you think St. John of the Cross meant when he said—in words Thérèse would have etched on her heart—that renunciation is the only lasting key to liberation?

2. How do you respond to those times when your best evangelizing efforts produce minimal to nonexistent results? Are you able to renounce your previous expectations and ask God for the courage to start again?

3. How can meditating on Thérèse's life and teaching help you to renounce such obstacles to evangelization

as willfulness ("My way or the highway") and specu-
lative thinking out of touch with reality?

Closing Prayer

Lord, teach me, in contrast to worldly power, the power-
lessness of the Cross. Let me renounce the illusion that I
can penetrate this mystery and believe with Thérèse that
"whenever I am weak, then I am strong" (2 Cor 12:10).
Teach me never to operate apart from your plan, mysterious as it may be. Show me that however challenging the
work of evangelization may be, it is best to renounce my
narrow views and trust that there is "time for every matter
under heaven" (Eccl 3:1). Amen.

8

The Little Way of Unceasing, World-Redeeming Prayer

Remember that on earth I want
To console you for the forgetfulness of sinners.
My only LOVE, grant my prayer.
Ah! Give me a thousand hearts to love you.
"Jesus, My Beloved, Remember!"[1]

As a Carmelite nun, Thérèse coped with what for her seemed an irreconcilable tension: How could a frail nun in a French cloister respond to the pressing call she felt within herself, the call to ecclesial evangelization within the universal Church:

> "I feel the *vocation* of the WARRIOR, THE PRIEST, THE APOSTLE, THE DOCTOR, THE MARTYR. Finally, I feel the need and the desire of carrying out the most heroic deeds for YOU, O Jesus. I feel within my soul the courage of the Crusader, the Papal Guard, and I would want to die on the field of battle in defense of the Church."[2]

How did she respond to this call? She committed herself to unceasing, world-redeeming prayer. By any standards, even for the bravest among us, this seems like a tall order. Thérèse wrote these words in the heat of her passion to

serve the Church as a member of Christ's Mystical Body
ought to do. While a woman of her youth and physical
weakness could not don the armor of a warrior king, was
it not part of her Carmelite vocation to be a soldier for
the Lord? The only arms she could carry were prayer and
fasting, but with these two weapons she knew she could
defeat the demonic and contribute to the redemption of
the world. Thérèse was moved to write:

> I feel in me the vocation of the PRIEST. With what love,
> O Jesus, I would carry You in my hands when, at my
> voice, You would come down from heaven. And with
> what love would I give You to souls! But alas! While
> desiring to be a *Priest*, I admire and envy the humility
> of St. Francis of Assisi and I feel the *vocation* of imitating
> him in refusing the sublime dignity of the *Priesthood*.[3]

This bold claim was not a plea to be ordained, which was
out of the question, but a longing to live to the full what
the Apostle Peter had proclaimed, "You are a chosen race,
a royal priesthood, a holy nation, God's own people, in
order that you may proclaim the mighty acts of him who
called you out of darkness into his marvelous light" (1 Pt
2:9). Her evangelical work would be to radiate the light of
faith in dark nights of unknowing, undefeated by disease
and frequent bouts of spiritual dryness. Bolstered by her
vowed life, she concelebrated with Jesus the core meanings
of evangelization. Every eucharistic service positioned
her to live the priestly ideal of decreasing that Christ may
increase. Every book she read challenged her to try harder
to be another Christ. Wearing his mantle drew her into the
realm of his royal priesthood and confirmed her call to
banish evil by doing good.

Among all of his worldwide travels to preach and teach, Fr. Adrian van Kaam often recounted his trip to the leper colony in Molokai. He was brought there by a Catholic dentist, who volunteered his time and skill to care as best he could for the dental hygiene of those afflicted with what was then thought to be an incurable disease requiring separation from non-infected people.

No sooner had Fr. Adrian gotten off the dentist's boat when one of the nuns expressed her joy in meeting him (she had read several of his books) and asked if he would accompany her to the room of a woman ravaged by the disease who had also come to know him because one of the sisters had read to her many passages from his books. Father agreed immediately.

The leper woman he met, though missing a nose and without fingers or toes, was, in his words, "one of the most beautiful women I ever met." She had a perfect set of teeth through which she strung her rosary beads hour after hour, praying for everyone in the colony and in the world who needed her intercession, praying to Jesus through Mary.

Fr. Adrian admitted that in his priestly life to date he had seldom been more evangelized than by this woman, who suffered without so much as a word of complaint.

To be counted among the Lord's most loyal followers the apostles themselves, his instruments of evangelization, was a thought Thérèse treasured. The action it required was to bring the joy of the Gospel into every corner of convent life. Her apostolate was in the cloister, but its effects were to be spread throughout the world. Through the power of the Holy Spirit, she proclaimed the Gospel by the life that she led. She invited her fellow Christians to touch Jesus in the flesh and to meet every obstacle on this evangelical path with courage. Thus she could say with conviction: "I have the *vocation of the Apostle*, I would like to travel over the whole earth to preach your name and to plant your glorious Cross on infidel soil. But, *O my Beloved*, one mission alone would not be sufficient for me. I would want to preach the Gospel on all five continents simultaneously and even to the most remote isles."[4] Nothing could stop Thérèse from praying for souls in the Far East, in Africa, in the Americas, or on the Continent. In one day she could bring Jesus to India, on the next to Australia. Geography was no match for the power of prayer!

Ah! Then to be a martyr! That, too, seemed within the range of her call to "shed my blood for you even to the very last drop."[5] She had dreamt about being a martyr since her youth. Amazingly, she found a way to realize this dream by making the distinction between martyrdom of blood, a sudden slaying for Jesus' sake, and martyrdom of desire, a day-by-day immolation. The latter turned out to be her lot:

> Like You, my Adorable Spouse, I would be scourged and crucified. I would die flayed like St. Bartholomew. I would be plunged into boiling oil like St. John; I would undergo all the tortures inflicted upon the martyrs. With St. Agnes and St. Cecilia, I would present my neck to the sword, and like Joan of Arc, my dear sister, I would whisper at the stake Your Name, O JESUS.[6]

The daily martyrdom Jesus willed for Thérèse meant that she could be an unblemished victim on the altar of love. She could go there without fear, for God had chosen her as a holocaust and turned her nothingness into fire.[7] Even silence, when she might have been dying to speak, became a way to proclaim the position Jesus took before his accusers (see Mt 27:14). The worth of Thérèse's missionary endeavors can be validated by the sheer number of churches that bear her name. Following her little way of spiritual childhood enables each of us to "go . . . and make disciples of all nations . . . teaching them to obey everything that I have commanded you" (Mt 28:19–20).

Sacrificing self for others' sake was another fruit of Thérèse's commitment to world-redeeming prayer. She never gave in to the temptation to stop praying amidst her suffering because she counted on the victory of Jesus in the depth of her soul. Because she was only capable of doing little things, she learned the greatest lesson of all: that at the heart of our evangelizing efforts is our identification with the paschal mystery, especially when we pray with the Publican, "God, be merciful to me, a sinner!" (Lk 18:13). Dying to self is the only way to experience what living for God really means. Even on her death bed, Thérèse knew that a soul burning with love could never be inactive. It might appear as if she were doing nothing, but Jesus was using her "loving audacity"[8] to attract others to himself. Is this not what being a missionary really means?

Thérèse's breathing may have gone into sporadic spasms, but prayer in tune with the breath of God never left her. As her days on earth came to a close, she felt that lasting rest would not be her lot as long as there was one soul left on earth to be saved. She had labored hard to live up to her evangelical call and she wanted to work just as diligently in paradise. Joining Jesus in his mission of redemption was a pledge on her part that united contemplation and action: "For me, *prayer* is an aspiration of the heart, it is a simple glance directed to heaven, it is a cry of gratitude and love in the midst of trial as well as joy;

finally it is something great, supernatural, which expands my soul and unites me to Jesus."[9]

To become instruments in Christ's hands, as Thérèse was, we must be willing to submit to the Master's instructions. He needs us to incarnate his redeeming plan, however limited in age or agility we may be. Although Thérèse's energy waned day after day, she expended what was available to her to complete her tasks. Jesus' redemptive mission was what mattered to her, not the fragile instrument he had chosen to execute it. Everything she did was done to please God. *The ministerial skill in which Thérèse excelled was that of inhaling God in prayer and exhaling his goodness in service.* Vulnerability did not deter the efficacy of her apostolate since any accomplishments she recorded in her diary were Christ's doing, not hers. Inner-directed as her prayer life was, it had a highly active component. No day passed when she did not beg God to reactivate his redeeming plan through her. How could death separate her from this pledge to apostolic love and service? After all, "she told God that she wanted all her prayers applied to sinners." To the novices, Thérèse said, "I am prepared to lay down my life for [You], but my affection is so pure that I don't want to attract [Your] hearts to me; I understand that my mission was to lead [you] to God. . . ."[10]

All Thérèse's prayers defocused on self and refocused on bringing the tenderness and compassion of Jesus to others in Carmel and in the wider world. It was as if her prayers and sacrifices passed through the convent walls to where God most needed them in the ongoing story of salvation. It was only through prayer and sacrifice that she knew she could be useful to the Church. While Thérèse could not have known what her destiny would be, she prayed that the message of love that captured the heart of her mission would never be lost. She believed that the projects she started on earth would continue in heaven. The redeeming mission of Jesus never ends, so why should hers? How could God have given her the desire of doing good on earth after her death had he not willed the way by which she would be able to realize it?

Eighth Facet of the New Evangelization

To join the whole Church in prayer for the world-redeeming mission Christ came to fulfill, praising his glory and thanking him in advance for the good he wills to accomplish through us.

Questions for Reflection

1. Why is prayer the firm foundation underlying any and all of the evangelizing tasks you may be called by God to fulfill?

2. St. Thérèse proclaimed the Gospel by the life she led through the power of the Holy Spirit. In what way do you do the same?

3. Is prayer for you, as it was for the saint of Lisieux, "an aspiration of the heart. . ." "a simple glance directed to heaven. . ." "a cry of gratitude and love in the midst of trial as well as joy"? How would you assess the relevance of these teachings of St. Thérèse on prayer in today's world?

Closing Prayer

Lord, open the ears of my heart in prayerful receptivity to the smallest whispers of your call. Let prayer be to my spirit what breath is to my body. Only then may the truth you ask me to proclaim guide and sustain my ministry. Let prayers of love cast out any lingering fears I may have about what the future holds. Thanks to the intercession of St. Thérèse, may I resist the temptations to stop praying amidst my suffering and count instead on the victory of Jesus in my soul. Amen.

9

The Little Way of Simplicity

I want sweetness and purity
To shine on your brow,
But the virtue that I give you
Above all is Simplicity.
"The Queen of Heaven to her Beloved Child. . . ."[1]

Before turning our attention to the grandeur of simplicity, let us review the first eight steps Thérèse has taught us as evangelizers in the Church. They may imprint themselves more indelibly upon us if we do so using the imperative tense:

1. Practice the efficacious witness of hiddenness.

2. Be grateful for the richness of the ordinary.

3. Count the blessings of trusting in Divine Mercy.

4. Live to the full your sacramental life.

5. Abandon yourself to the providence of God.

6. Experience friendship with God and others.

7. Renounce your selfishness and follow Jesus.

8. Engage in the little way of unceasing, world-redeeming prayer.

Now we are ready to consider why simplicity is so important.

There is a trend that tells us to simplify everything from meal preparation to home furnishings. Too much stuff takes more time than we want to invest to care for it. Perhaps this recommendation is a reaction to the phenomenon of "too muchness." How many rooms can two people really occupy? Aren't three televisions (one in the living room, one in the den, one in the master bedroom) enough? And so it goes. . . .

The urge to simplify a life that has become far too complicated was brought home to me on an evening in southwest Florida when I was one of the many guests invited to a dinner party hosted by a benefactor of a local art gallery where the work of a friend of mine was on display.

Tired of the "cocktail party" chatter, I found myself out on his waterfront deck getting some fresh air. I turned to catch the last rays of the sun, only to notice that our host was beside me and asked if we might have a word. Obviously my friend had told him of my work in the ministry of faith formation, which made him sure, in his words, that I was trustworthy. He asked me to look at the end of the deck at the two luxury yachts docked there. I said they were truly amazing, reminding me more of a movie set than of a private person's possessions. Looking at me with eyes slightly downcast, he said in a low voice, "That's the point. My life is overwhelmed by having to keep track of these yachts, let alone everything else I own. I've been asking myself, 'After all, how many yachts can I water-ski behind?' Do you see what I mean?" I nodded in the affirmative and then another guest put her arm in his and escorted him away. I thought of the three-word directive I had read years ago in Henry David Thoreau's masterpiece *Walden*, "Simplify, simplify, simplify." That was my silent prayer for this lost soul.

No one would doubt the complexity of life in today's world, but even in Carmel life could contradict the ideal of simplicity. Within the enclosure, as well as in family life and society, one could find signs of vainglory, envy, anger, and subtle forms of avarice, as seemingly innocuous as hoarding bits of string and snippets of wrapping paper. How to foster this key virtue of evangelical witness was a lesson Jesus taught Thérèse in a charming way:

> He set before her the book of nature; she understood how all the flowers he has created are beautiful, how the splendor of the rose and the whiteness of the lily do not take away the perfume of the little violet or the delightful simplicity of the daisy. She understood that if all flowers wanted to be roses, nature would lose her springtime beauty, and the fields would no longer be decked out with little wild flowers.[2]

Beneath the vast variety to be found in the world of nature, Thérèse saw the unifying love of our Creator. Diversity ought not to divide us from the underlying oneness mystics like Thérèse behold. Incarnating God's will in all that we say and do is one of the uncomplicated fruits of Christian evangelization. Simplicity means celebrating the transcendent in the here and now. It means detecting deeper truths in faith where others see only reasons to doubt. To be simple is to wait upon reality as it is, not to filter its ambiguity through the narrow viewfinder of our own, often overly complex, expectations.

Simple means uncomplicated, lacking in guile, seeing with eyes of faith, the often invisible good we seek to foster. If life can be at times like a dense forest overgrown with the dry underbrush of confusion and doubt, then simplicity is like a beam of light pointing to God's wisdom and truth. When she first read the writings of St. John of the Cross, Thérèse may not have understood them intellectually, but she certainly grasped their meaning in the simplicity of her heart. She allowed his words to fertilize, so to speak, the already experienced ground of her conversion to Christ. They lessened her fear to enter into the midnight moments of naked faith, hope, and love. Her simple goal in Carmel was to remain in God's presence with the prayer of loving attention at the forefront of her consciousness. This stance allowed her to listen to the Father whenever and however he chose to speak to her through the Holy Spirit. What followed from this simple act of seeing were gentle attempts to respond to the grace God initiated and to avoid any complicated efforts to attain self-willed perfection.

A good starting point on the way to expressing an exemplary life of evangelization is to begin with a simple, accepting assessment of the truth that our whole being ought to be an embodiment of God's eternal, infinite love for souls. Ours is the business of holy living and holy dying, whether like Thérèse we are pruning the rose bushes in our garden or lying in a hospital bed with barely enough strength to utter a simple "yes" to God. And yet, that one word contains a whole alphabet of love for him and others. Once said, it gives God permission to edit the story of our life for his honor and glory.

Thérèse teaches us in simple yet profound ways that the purpose of existence is to become who God wants us to be with much less effort than we thought possible. She joins the company of contemplatives who excelled in saving the world without denying in the least the fact that it was in a state of enmity to God. Too much concentration on complexity only leads to more confusion. Keep it simple. Focus on the duty of the present moment and do your best to bring souls to Jesus. For Thérèse, simplicity of soul and unity of will were two sides of the same coin. As one of the older sisters told her: "Your soul is extremely *simple*, but when you will be perfect, you will be even more *simple* [because] the closer one approaches God, the simpler one becomes."[3] Such is the grandeur of simplicity. Thérèse disengaged herself from any and all prideful preoccupations that tended to shatter the unifying nature of her call. She developed an evangelizing heart by decentering from any memory, imagination, or anticipation not in conformity with the commandments Christ's every action confirmed.

Willfulness makes it impossible to live the little way of spiritual childhood. Think of how tense and unpleasant life becomes when we go on the defensive, feel weighed down by convoluted arguments, and long for the light-heartedness bestowed on us by such dispositions of discipleship as poverty of spirit and purity of heart. Christ wants to free us from all traces of petty stubbornness and erratic emotionality so that we can enjoy the simple in-flowing of Divine Grace. This intention in itself does not make us holy, but it does soften the hard edges encrusted in our fallen condition. Thanks to the gift of simplicity associated with spiritual childhood, we may enjoy the double effect of radiating Christ's presence wherever we are and in whatever we do. The rhythm of life to which we adhere consists of an outer movement of incarnation by which we embody Christian virtues and an inner movement of contemplation by which we replenish them.

The second childhood of St. Thérèse is nothing short of remarkable. It exemplifies not only her state of life after her Christmas conversion but our own and anyone's return to our inmost origins in God. After years of experience—good and not so good—we long to taste in time what we trust we will savor in eternity. Simplicity leads us to a complete identification with Christ and through him with the family of the Trinity; it is the magnet that attracts to itself such virtues as trust, patience, docility, gentleness, and firmness. We look at the diverse aspects of evangelization with a singleness of eye that solidifies our own commitment to life itself as one act of love. This simple yet profound trait bolstered Thérèse's ability to face situations that by merely human standards seemed insurmountable.

An experience I once had at the shore on a hot summer day may shed light on this simple goal of grateful acceptance. I rested on my beach towel and felt the warm sand under it. The beauty of sea, sun, and sky delighted the eye. I meditated on how everything hung together in perfect harmony. Then, for whatever reason, I undertook a kind of imaginative excursion. I began to mix these elements up in a chaotic, colorful, intertwined but totally complex and unorganized way as if they were ingredients in a fast speeding blender. The effect frightened me. There was a riot of form and matter but no order. I shut the blender off and took a deep breath. I let the parts of this lustrous scene return to what they were: not a shapeless blend but an ordered connection as profound as it was simple. Just the sea. Just the sun. Just the sky. All fulfilling their proper end in the symphony of goodness, truth, and beauty orchestrated by God. How gracious he was to give me a fresh glimpse into the essential coherence, the simple togetherness of all that is.

Simplicity is grand because it holds in place the pure intention to let God's providential care suffuse our whole being. His love-will directs our every intention and action. Simplicity sends out a warning signal when we are inclined to forfeit the grace of childlikeness in favor of allowing little gods of our own making to gain ascendancy. Similarly, the self-knowledge gained through experiences of success and failure, of delight and disappointment, put to rest complex questions for which there are no answers. We acknowledge our weakness and wait upon God as our strength. Jesus gave Thérèse the privilege of penetrating into the mysterious depths of these profound truths. Since she had no capacity to express this "heavenly melody," God had to be content with the "stammerings of a little child"[4] whose simplicity seemed as pleasing to him as the symphony of the spheres.

Throughout this telling of her story, Thérèse encourages us to simplify our lives by putting to rest the functionalistic pressures that chronically complicate them. Meetings start to happen less frequently and for shorter time periods. Not every email we receive has to be answered right away. We cease trying to control everything in favor of simply enjoying the exquisite work our Creator accomplished in those original seven days so magnificently depicted at the beginning of the book of Genesis.

Thérèse teaches us by example how to walk in the truth of who we are: children of God endowed with the simple task of adoring our Lord and Master contemplatively while acting in accordance with what he asks of us.

One sure benefit of simplicity is better seeing. We become centered in our Creator instead of losing ourselves in the created. This worshipful attitude, far from removing us from the cares of this world, far from lessening our evangelical efficiency, enables us to be more present and productive. Because we are less tense and uptight, we can flow with the situation at hand and accomplish the mission entrusted to us.

Ninth Facet of the New Evangelization

To simplify our lives enough to see what God needs us to do rather than slavishly following our own agenda and risking to complicate the pristine goodness, truth, and beauty of the Divine Plan.

Questions for Reflection

1. Is there something in your life you would like to simplify? How might you go about doing so?

2. What inclines you to filter your life through your own, often complex, expectations? Is it possible to change your heart and change your life by simply waiting upon reality as it comes from the hand of God and then appraising what to do?

3. In what way does the virtue of simplicity prevent you from forfeiting the grace of childlikeness in favor of the functionalistic pressures that complicate your life?

Closing Prayer

Lord, help me to understand the simple yet profound mystery of your transforming love in my life. Give me the courage to uncomplicate what stands in the way of my *yes* to your call. Let me see with eyes of faith the wisdom of remaining in your presence in the simplest way possible. However unworthy I am, grant me the grace of joining the company of contemplatives who, like St. Thérèse, attracted souls to Jesus by the sheer goodness they displayed. Amen.

10

The Little Way of Freedom

Looking for pure joy and true freedom. . . .
Spreading good deeds was her delight,
And forgetting herself, her only wish. . . .
"The Portrait of a Soul I Love"[1]

Who of us does not want to be in the know? We are wired by the media to receive information.

What was she whispering about?

What was behind the speech he made at that meeting?

Where is she going now? With whom?

Why did he look at me that way?

Will she ever calm down and listen?

At least overtly, our aim is not to meddle in others' lives, but still we make that call or ask that question. Speculation and the useless worry it engenders can exhaust the energy we need to pursue Christian excellence in the working places of family, Church, and society. Being worldly bound turns our attention away from God. Idle curiosity takes precedence over prayer. Meddling can give rise to envy and jealousy, especially in the close confines of a parish or community. Gossip may begin to buzz around like flies in an open-air restaurant, annoying everyone. Ministers of the Gospel get more involved in one another's business than in the business of the Lord, creating a bad climate for ministry.

Several years ago, in the midst of my academic career and after I had received a full tenured professorship at the university where I taught, I was asked, as is the custom, to sit on the tenure committee. We met regularly to review future applicants. What disturbed me was the trend to "publish or perish." Those granted tenure (I had published!) were assessed in the light of the accomplishments listed on their résumé (grants, publications, memberships), which was all well and good, but too often professors were bypassed who may not have written a major book in their field, at least not yet and perhaps based on their expertise maybe never, but who were among the best teachers I knew. They were the ones who always had time to talk to their students, to help them write their papers, to lead them to the threshold of their true calling. The tenure climate veered more toward measurement than toward meaning and at times became so judgmental that I respectfully asked to resign. Even then, I found myself pondering what it meant to be and become another Christ for others, especially the most vulnerable among us.

Like explorers finding a secret map to a gold mine, so was Thérèse led by the Spirit to uncover one of the secrets of the mystical life, revealing the epicenter of true evangelization. The paradox she experienced was that only when we are *bound* to Christ are we truly *free*. In the Carmelite tradition, many masters who preceded her concurred that renunciation of our false self is the key to liberation of our true self.

This paradox pervades the *Story of a Soul*. From both John of the Cross and Teresa of Ávila, whose works guided her formation, Thérèse learned how to approach the darkest of nights as an invitation to grow in knowledge of herself and God: "Ah! How many lights have I not drawn from the works of our holy father, St. John of the Cross! At the age of seventeen and eighteen, I had no other spiritual nourishment. . . ."[2] St. John taught her to see meaning in every moment—including when, toward the end of her life, she felt bereft of consolation.

Having trained herself to cling to Jesus, Thérèse trusted that this sinking feeling that God is absent does not last forever. Having refused to make ultimate anyone or anything less than God, she enjoyed the freedom to put into practice another divine directive she learned from the Carmelite masters—that the key to holiness resides in nothingness! This acknowledgment of our nothingness provides the spiritual nourishment we need to persevere in spreading the message of the Gospel by means of the proclamation, witness, and worship that accompany faith deepening.

Because of her youth and the fragile state of her health, Thérèse had no choice but to accept that her spiritual growth required permission from her superiors from having to follow to the letter a multiplicity of rules and mortifications; its ground had to be the self-renunciation that made her a joyful prisoner of the Lord. The reward of being bound to him was a peace beyond words wherein her sole desire was to unite her will with his.

As her illness progressed, she adopted the habit of underlining texts that dealt with the death to self through love. Perhaps she read passages like this one from the *Sayings of Light and Love* of St. John of the Cross:

> The very pure spirit does not bother about the regard of others or human respect, but communes inwardly

with God, alone and in solitude as to all forms, and
with delightful tranquility, for the knowledge of God is
received in divine silence.[3]

It was as if God's grace led her beyond intellectual understanding to a way of living the mystery of being bound yet
free. It was as if St. John said to her personally: "Since God
is inaccessible, be careful not to concern yourself with all
that your faculties can comprehend and your senses feel,
so that you do not become satisfied with less and lose the
lightness of soul suitable for going to him."[4] In the end,
Thérèse was left with no other task than to seek God with
a pure and selfless love. She was freed from the fear of
death and saw it as nothing more than a passage to new
life. Guided by St. John, all she had left to say was: "O
sweetest love of God, so little known, whoever has found
this rich mine is at rest!"[5]

The freedom of being bound to Christ prepares us to
be evangelizers who, like Thérèse, want *to be love* at the
heart of the Church. The apostolic message proclaimed by
St. Paul, that the victory belongs to Jesus (see 1 Cor 15:50),
becomes a reservoir of wisdom impossible to empty. When
she was at her weakest, Thérèse found the strength to welcome death as the way through which Jesus would allow
her to save innumerable souls. At the very time when she
was a prisoner of her body, her soul was freer than ever
to soar to the heights of discipleship. All Jesus asked was
that she trust in him and hold nothing of herself in reserve.
As St. John confirms: "When evening comes, you will be
examined in love. Learn to love as God desires to be loved
and abandon your own ways of acting."[6]

What better description could have been found to
depict the state of a soul purified and perfected by grace?

In the nights of self-renunciation, God accomplishes what a soul overly attached to the ways of the world could never do. We begin to awaken from the illusion that lesser goods on display in the windows of power, pleasure, and possession can ever satisfy our longing for God. Faced with bombardments that promise fast and lasting fulfillment, we rebind spirit, heart, mind, and will to the Lord and loosen ourselves from the allure of idolizing these false gods.

In the dark nights of sense and spirit that inevitably shadow both worship and witness, we may feel stripped to the bone of our being, but we have no doubt that God will guide us to that place of grace where the peace and joy of Christ prevails: "For this slight momentary affliction is preparing us for an eternal weight of glory beyond all measure, because we look not at what can be seen but at what cannot be seen; for what cannot be seen is eternal" (2 Cor 4:17–18).

The more we ponder the paradox of liberation through renunciation, the more we see that in these nights of the soul new light shines forth. All of our senses—seeing, hearing, touching, tasting, smelling—are accommodated to our spirit and disposed by God for the union of love that is our destiny. God does this work of forming, reforming, and transforming our souls actively and passively on one condition—that we hold nothing of ourselves in reserve.

This is a hard lesson for a busy person like myself to learn. Many a time I have come to the end of a long day of writing, teaching, and office work and with briefcase in hand and car keys out of my purse, headed for the parking lot, only to hear a tap on the door and a request I had hoped at that moment not to hear, "Doctor Muto, may I have a minute of your time?" Of course, I realize that this does not mean sixty seconds. I nod in assent and we both sit down. I ask, "How can I help you?" and for the next half hour I listen, nod in understanding, and say something like, "I see" or "go on, please." Finally, the encounter I had least wanted to engage in comes to a courteous close. I thank her for sharing her concerns so openly, promise to keep her in my prayers (which I do), and regather my things to drive home. A few days later, we see each other in the hallway and, much to my embarrassment, she runs up to tell me that "our time together was the best ever and that her problems seem to have disappeared." I smile and say to myself, "But you did nothing except to listen." Then I beg the Lord to receive the compliments she had just paid to me.

The virtue of self-relinquishment is the subsoil of evangelical dedication. Life around us becomes more courteous than controlled and more good work is accomplished. Charity and compassion replace contempt and competition. Backbiting is impossible when we bind ourselves to the Beloved. When turmoil threatens to disrupt tranquility, we return to that quiet center where time spent with God becomes time well spent.

When Thérèse wrote her act of oblation to merciful love, she had dropped every iota of self-centeredness. Guided by grace, she could say:

> In order to live in one single act of perfect love, I OFFER MYSELF AS A VICTIM OF HOLOCAUST TO YOUR MERCIFUL LOVE, asking you to consume me incessantly, allowing the waves of *infinite* tenderness shut up within you to overflow into my soul, and that thus I may become A MARTYR OF YOUR LOVE. O My God![7]

Just when Thérèse wanted to be swept up in the radiance of the empty tomb, she entered the maelstrom of bodily malfunction. She had no other recourse than to interpret every breakdown she experienced as a call from her Divine Spouse. He alone could give her the chance to dispel all doubts and breakthrough to the mountaintop of naked faith, which is the only proximate means to union with God. As the mist that surrounded her ascent became thicker, the mystery of transforming love penetrated her soul. Sweet images of the homeland gave way to imageless longing. Only in the final moments before her death did this cloud lift a little. Any bliss she felt came from blind faith. The last words she spoke to Mother Marie de Gonzague were these:

> "O mother. I assure you, the chalice is filled to the brim!"
> "God is surely not going to abandon me!"
> "He has never abandoned me before!"[8]

Tenth Facet of the New Evangelization

To show believers and sincere seekers that being bound to Christ is the only way to free oneself from the illusion that lesser goods can fulfill our longing for the greater good that is God.

Questions for Reflection

1. Can you recall an experience when useless worry curtailed your freedom and exhausted your energy? How can you avoid such a drain emotionally and spiritually in the future?

2. Are you comfortable with the mystical paradox that only when you yoke yourself to Christ can you be truly free? If not, why not?

3. What "false gods" do you still chase after as sources of fulfillment? How can you escape the entrapment of these inordinate attachments and pursue as central the goods only God can give?

Closing Prayer

Lord, inspired by the example of St. Thérèse, let me find the secrets of the mystical life that open the floodgates of lasting evangelization. Yoke me to yourself so that I may be free to do your work in and with my faith community. Let me say with all the saints, "I am nothing. You are all." Fulfill my longing for that peace beyond words that comes only when my will and yours are one. Loosen me from the allure of worldliness that shadows my witness to you. Take me to that quiet center where time spent with you is the key to spending time in service of you. Amen.

11

The Little Way of Purgation, Illumination, and Union

Jesus, holy and sacred Vine,
O my divine King, you know
I am a cluster of golden grapes
Which must disappear for you.
Under the wine press of suffering,
I shall prove my love for you
I want no other joy
Than to sacrifice myself each day.
"My Desires Near Jesus. . . ."[1]

Each step along the way lived and taught by St. Thérèse of Lisieux leads to yet another intriguing facet of evangelical commitment. A map familiar to her would have been the threefold path of purgation, illumination, and union. It traces our following of Christ from the Mount of Calvary to the light of Tabor to the glory of Easter morn. Patience in suffering, trust in God's providence, and self-sacrificing love and service of others enable us to endure and pass beyond the setbacks evangelization may entail.

By keeping the end stage of union with God in mind from the beginning, we avoid exposing ourselves to the demonic ploys of depletion and discouragement. Egocentric temptations give way to Christocentric dependence on the mystery of forming, reforming, and transforming love. This initial purgation of our self-centered pride leads to a clearer illumination of who we are and of what God wants us to do. As our love for the Trinity expands and intensifies, we shed the last remnants of willfulness and enter into the core meaning of discipleship. "I have been crucified with Christ; and it is no longer I who live, but it is Christ who lives in me" (Gal 2:19–20).

Repeated acts of self-abandonment carry us over the hurdles of spiritual desolation. Sooner than later, obedience to the divine initiative becomes our chief concern. As Thérèse herself discovered: "O Jesus, my Beloved who could express the tenderness and sweetness with which You are guiding my soul! It pleases You to cause the rays of Your grace to shine through even in the midst of the darkest storm!"[2]

Keeping the balance between darkness and light is not easy. Evangelizing efforts cause us to walk the razor's edge between being too active or too passive, too pushy or too lethargic, overly careful or inexcusably careless. Our aim is to experience God's presence in us and in everything we do. We take steps to progress on the threefold path, but regression can occur. What then? Thérèse offers this answer:

> The little flower transplanted to Mount Carmel was to expand under the shadow of the cross. The tears and blood of Jesus were to be her dew and her Sun was His adorable Face veiled with tears. Until my coming to Carmel, I had never fathomed the depths of the treasures hidden in the Holy Face.[3]

To live under the shadow of the Cross, in awe of Jesus' bloody yet benign expression of pure love, gives us a heightened sense of being held close to his heart, no matter what demands the work of evangelization make upon us. The purgative path cleanses our way of seeing below the surface of mundane endeavors to a deeper meaning. The night may be dark, but when we look again, we detect a laser beam of redeeming love.

Tests of our fidelity to the Gospel are never lacking in daily life. They remind us that purgation is not a stopping point along the way to union but an ongoing process. Thérèse probably felt its purifying effects in the sheer drudgery of each day: another bed to make, another corridor to sweep, another potato to peel. Similar routines are known to all of us. Their importance lies in the fact that they teach us not to look elsewhere for fulfillment but to strive to find it here-and-now.

It is 4:30 in the afternoon and I have guests coming for dinner at 6:30 sharp. I have planned the moves I had to make to be ready for them. I'm in the supermarket fifteen minutes later, shopping list in hand. On it I have listed exactly twelve items so that I can go swiftly through the express lane and be at home in time to prepare the meal I want to serve. All goes well until I find myself behind a person who has fifteen items in her basket! I can count, can't I?

I feel that first surge of impatience rising to a fever pitch when, instead of paying for her items in cash, which the sign on the express lane tells her to do, she has to write a check, and, of course, someone from the office has to be called to approve it. Now I'm fifteen minutes behind my schedule, knowing I have a choice to make: do I cave in to the "demon of impatience" or do I turn to the Lord of Lords in prayer? I know it was the power of the Holy Spirit that enabled me to let go of my schedule and flow with whatever God wanted. I said a little prayer for the person in front of me as she thanked the clerk profusely and went on her way. As it turned out, my guests were late and I had plenty of time to set the table and cook what they said was a delicious meal. Never had grace before it been so beautiful to me!

Purifying formation is not an end in itself but a step along the way to illuminating reformation and unifying transformation. Pinpricks of purification may be as non-descript as an occasional case of sleeplessness or having to wake up and bathe on a cold day when the hot water tank breaks. There is no way to escape every affliction, from annoying inconveniences to terminal illnesses. Affliction is part of the human condition, not a strike against us by an uncaring God. Purifying formation cancels the illusion that we are sufficient unto ourselves. In the midst of afflic-tion's fire, we aspire toward union with God: "My one purpose, then, would be to accomplish the will of God, to sacrifice myself for Him in the way that would please Him."[4]

God proved to Thérèse more than once that suffering is a blessing in disguise. It purifies self-pity and arouses compassion for our own and others' vulnerability. What better reasons could there be for suffering than to remind us of our creaturehood and to teach us to love others as we love ourselves. The purification process is not an exercise in passivity; we have an active role to play. Thérèse did so by following the rules pertaining to fasting and absti-nence; by setting aside time for prayer and meditation;

and by detaching herself from whatever stood between her and God, especially the volatility of her own emotions.

The purifying action of God's grace makes such detachment possible, but we have to cooperate with it every time someone tries our patience or disappoints our expectations. Unreasonable reactions, cantankerous behavior, raised eyebrows, and chiding frowns are stings we must learn to welcome as part of the training we need to live and teach the Gospel. Their aim is to purify traces of self-pity, anger, and depression.

Day after day God purges our souls of any affection or attachment that threatens our primary relationship with him or tempts us to settle for trivia. Many daily dyings have to be undergone for Christ's sake. Our place in this process is to accept them without complaint; they are more than mere inconveniences or trifling losses. They enable us to let go of our own impulses and to admit how silly it is to complain. On this purgative path to evangelical excellence, we learn to accept interruptions as inspirations; we pause for prayer before we rush to judgment; we listen before leaping to a wrong conclusion; we maintain inner calm amidst outer trials. The fruits of purgation are God-centeredness and preservation of his peace in and around us.

Thérèse wanted Jesus to use her as an instrument "to carry on His work in souls."[5] She delighted in the truth of this revelation: "What do you have that you did not receive? And if you received it, why do you boast as if it were not a gift? Already you have all you want! Already you have become rich!" (1 Cor 4:7–8). She sought the last place because that is what Jesus would have done. What mattered to her was becoming poor for Christ's sake.

Such poverty of spirit entails a sincere commitment not to covet any goods nor to forfeit the joy only being possessed by God can bring: "For a long time I have not belonged to myself since I delivered myself totally to Jesus, and He is therefore free to do with me as He pleases."[6] Such inner cleansing results in our choosing to be of service to God by being faithful in little things.

I must again thank my maternal grandmother Elizabeth for teaching me this lesson. Her life canceled any possibility of grandiose plans and projects, but her love for littleness taught me what it takes to purge our ego of every tendency toward self-aggrandizement.

When she moved to the home where she would live and die, she announced to the neighbors that she would plant a garden and share her produce with them. They laughed. Nothing grew on these mud-caked hillsides where long ago people mined coal. They did not know my grandmother nor her intimate relationship with the Lord. I knew that she would tell him in the purity of her peasant faith that she wanted to plant a garden full of vegetables and deliver them to neighbors in need. She probably said to him in Italian, "Please move this uncultivated clay. It's like a mountain!" To this prayer, I feel sure the Lord replied, "No problem. I'm happy to do this little favor for you."

It did not surprise me that at the end of the growing season, she went from door to door with baskets of green beans, homegrown lettuce, fresh basil, and juicy tomatoes. Without one word, she taught her young granddaughter the meaning of the Beatitude promising the pure of heart that they will see God (see Mt 5:8).

As our human nature passes through the process of purifying formation, we may feel like a log thrown on the fire that exudes heat as it is being consumed. It is as if God's love burns away the resistances to grace caused by impatience and egocentric choices while allowing our true being to reveal itself. We enter the illuminative way when we realize how much our inner sight has improved. For example, we spot like a hawk the subtle signs of egoism and its devious trappings. What we used to think of as important does not have the same priority. Invisible to the eyes of the world but visible to those of faith are the threads of Gospel truth being woven by the Lord into the fabric of our daily life. We see the beauty in all that God has created; we behold his face behind every apparent form.

The more we empty our intellect, memory, and will of misinterpretations and selfish desires, the more clarity of sight we gain. The shadows of our old ways, having been dispelled by the mercy of God, give way to the coming of the dawn. When pressures mount, we place ourselves in his presence. Now that the eyes of our interiority have been opened, we behold ourselves as children of God bound together by membership in the Mystical Body. We glimpse God's holy plans for our life and celebrate its inner coherence. Behind every tempest, we see a clear blue sky. Beneath the turbulence, we behold the calm of the ocean's floor.

Our illumined soul rests in God for however short or long a duration God allows, provided we do not resist or refuse this grace. Even when the felt sense of his presence recedes, our faith grows stronger. We return to our indwelling in the Holy Trinity and from there derive the strength we need to go forward. One by one, we reduce our manifold desires to a single-hearted longing for union with God. We want the insignificant streamlet we are to enter the Sea of Love from whence we came: In the spirit of Thérèse, we come to realize this awesome truth: "For is there a *joy* greater than that of suffering out of love for You? The more interior the suffering is and the less apparent to the eyes of creatures, the more it rejoices You, O my God!"[7]

The detachment of the purgative way frees us for greater attachment to the illuminative way. Arid and rainy seasons alternate in the spiritual life as they ebb and flow in any garden. That rhythm will not disconcert us as long as we strive to practice equanimity by keeping our eyes fixed on God. As Thérèse discovered, grace often prefers to work in the darkness of not knowing to draw us closer to God. Though we might wish for deliverance, we must not set our heart on it. Much to our amazement, God is not done with us yet. He is still in the process of readying our soul to be a receptacle for the gift of union with him.

Gazing at the gateway of unifying transformation teaches us not to trust ourselves but to trust wholly in the Lord. Evangelizers learn not to get in the way of God's guiding light, lest they be engulfed again by the tentacles of human pride. Purifying formation and illuminating reformation lead us to the portal of union with God, who alone enables us to enter into the land of likeness to the Trinity, freed from the burden of self-love.

In the evening of her life, these glimpses of union showed Thérèse mystical secrets impossible for words to disclose. Not even poetry could properly express the sublime encounter of remaining unique while being united with God. In the core of her being, God drew Thérèse to himself in silent love until it was time for him to lift her into his eternal embrace. In her tattered frame, light shone forth. That peace of soul only the Lord himself can grant enabled her to practice the virtue of "holy indifference" to everything, save obedience to his will. In possessing nothing, she came to possess all. Now only a gossamer veil separated her from God. Soon it would part and her consummation would be complete.

Just as she had trusted her vowed life to protect her from getting entangled in endless debates, so she trusted her Father in heaven to lift her through the love of his Son to new heights of Spirit-filled wisdom. She had known the twilight of purgation, the darkness of illumination, and the dawn of union. The sufferings God asked her to undergo were as nothing compared to her reception of the peace Jesus promised. She was a daughter of the Church, who flung herself with childlike abandonment into the embrace of the Triune God and who beheld behind every cloud a rainbow of faith, hope, and love:

> Ineffable abandonment! Divine melody!
> You disclose your love through your celestial song.
> Love that fears not, that falls asleep and forgets itself
> On the heart of God, like a little child. . . .[8]

Eleventh Facet of the New Evangelization

To open ourselves by the grace of God to the threefold path of purifying formation, illuminating reformation, and unifying transformation so that we may be led to the heart of discipleship by becoming *alter Christus*, another Christ.

Questions for Reflection

1. In the light of these foundational, formative teachings, are you willing to be led, if God so ordains, into the times of trial associated with purifying formation and illuminating reformation?

2. What in you has to be transformed to clear the way to the pursuit on your part of lasting evangelical excellence?

3. Do you try to die a little daily to your selfish ways in loving response to Christ's invitation to become more like him?

Closing Prayer

Lord, show me day by day how to follow you from the Mount of Calvary to the glory of Easter morn. Form, reform, and transform my life to welcome the setbacks and successes evangelization always entails. Grant me the grace to shed the last remnants of willfulness and enter into the core meaning of discipleship. Let obedience to your truth and your teaching become my chief concern. Please help me to resist any affection or attachment that threatens my primary love relationship with you. Amen.

12

The Little Way of Living in, with, and through the Lord in a Mystical Martyrdom of Love

Oh! What a sweet martyrdom.
I burn with love.
To you I sigh, Jesus, each day!
"The Atom of the Sacred Heart"[1]

In this era of evangelization, God calls each of us (laity, clergy, and religious) to exemplify and pass on to the next generation a legacy of living in, with, and through the Lord. By human standards, God's choice of Thérèse to be an exemplar of evangelization might seem foolhardy, but then God's ways are not our own. He himself chose the Cross as the instrument of our redemption. We may question the logic of such actions, but we cannot doubt their lasting fruits. Honesty about her own limits prompted Thérèse to admit that she was capable of disobeying God's slightest nod, but she refused to do so. Embedded in the legacy of her reflections on the meaning of suffering is the powerful witness provided by her mystical martyrdom of love. The Lord did not require of her anything extraordinary beyond her fidelity to follow the little way by which everyone could witness the presence of Jesus in her heart and in her apostolic works:

> God shows me clearly, however, without my perceiving it, the way to please Him and to practice the most sublime virtues. I have frequently noticed that Jesus doesn't want me to lay up *provisions*, He nourishes me at each moment with a totally new food; I find it within me without my knowing how it is there. I believe it is Jesus Himself hidden in the depths of my poor little heart: He is giving me the graces of acting within me, making me think of all He desires me to do at the present moment.[2]

What Thérèse discovered in the course of pleasing Jesus and practicing virtue was that she could serve him in the nearness of Lisieux just as well as others who gave their life for him to evangelize unbelievers in far off lands. Some are to serve Jesus among the homeless on city streets while others by preaching to regular church-goers in places of worship the world over.

Thérèse's chief assignment was to pray for those soldiers of Christ, who like her, had no "great desires except that of loving to the point of dying for love."[3] She encouraged those with whom she corresponded not to overlook the lofty graces that flowed from ordinary tasks done in self-forgetful love. Giving God love for love—that was the best way to please the Beloved in all things. In that sense, the obedience required of her revealed the legacy of Gospel living that Christ asked her to bestow on her sisters in Carmel as well as on the universal Church.

Living in, with, and through the Lord is the impetus behind effective evangelizing. When contemplation is the ground of action, we avoid the pitfalls of either pietism or activism. We accept our littleness and acknowledge that it is Jesus who accomplishes everything; we are but instruments in his hands. At day's end, we gather together any loose fragments of self that have inadvertently been loosened from him, apologize for this foolishness, and promise to do better tomorrow. Provided that we try not to deviate from this simple outflow of love, we will find the stamina needed to fulfill every duty assigned to us.

In learning to listen with the inner ears of faith, our functional attempts to figure things out (signed, sealed, and delivered) give way to a deeper empathy with and attention to what is being asked of us on a more profound level than the rational mind alone can grasp. By quieting our analytical intellect and its need to know everything— from initial plans to calculated outcomes—and trying instead to minister in, with, and through Christ, we may find released in us clearer forces of reflection and a depth of understanding ego intelligence alone cannot attain. How often in scripture does what appears to us as sheer foolishness reveal the depth and breadth of the wisdom of God?

That capacity to persevere joyfully in the ministry assigned to him by the Lord was what edified me and everyone who came in contact with Fr. Adrian van Kaam. Despite his fragile health, after his heart attack and open heart surgery, he listened to what he called in his book, *The Music of Eternity*, the everyday sounds of fidelity. He strove to obey the call disclosed to him by the mystery day by day over a lifetime. He embodied this call in his commitment to serve the Church and to address especially the needs of the people of God for always, ongoing, in-depth faith formation. By "always" he meant that our journey to the heart of the Trinity never ends, not in this lifetime or beyond. By "ongoing" he insisted that we must continue to listen to the invitations, challenges, and appeals communicated in the core of our being by the Holy Spirit. By "in-depth" he meant that we must never equate our formative spirituality with external devotions; rather we have to plunge with the help of grace into those deep waters of forming, reforming, and transforming love that surround us like the air we breathe.

Such listening, situated in the darkness of not knowing, calls for a suspension, at least momentarily, of our usual ways of comprehending and reflecting. This suspension requires that we let go of whatever images we have of God so that we can place ourselves in his presence and be ready to hear his voice in the center of our being. It would be a mistake to conclude that this suspension of our usual way of knowing makes us become merely passive receivers of a ministerial assignment, so far up in the clouds of transcendence that we are no longer in touch with the needs of the people around us.

In fact, the opposite is true. Quieting the mind results in a better grasp of what God asks of us in the context of daily reality. Stillness grants us greater awareness of the divine directives communicated by God to us in the here-and-now. We heed our present circumstances as conveyors of providential concern. Revealed thereby is a vein of meaning far richer than our isolated ego could have discerned.

Jesus works within us in a mysterious manner, inspiring our daily actions and uncomplicating our life. Thérèse convinces us that sanctity is not dependent on exalted experiences or spectacular achievements. It is the legacy of all baptized souls working together to reveal God's honor and glory and to provide excellent evangelizing tools for everyone. Like Thérèse, we, too, can show (without showing off!) that even the tiniest spark of love may burst into a roaring fire when we serve God with tenderness and tenacity. We are less bound to our narrow expectations of what should be and more present to the situation as coming from his hand.

Thérèse found that the easiest way to bolster her courage was to recall that "my one purpose would be to accomplish the will of God, to sacrifice myself for Him in the way that would please Him."[4] When anything beyond her control occurred, it was for her an invitation to trust all the more in God's outpouring of actual and sanctifying graces. She believed that her life offered ample proof that God is always there to pick us up when we fall down since we are too weak to walk alone. Penetrating to "the mysterious depths of charity"[5] revealed her own imperfections and forbade her to call attention to those bumps and bruises she saw in others. To love everyone as Jesus loved them was the Christian ideal that expanded her heart and created around her a climate of joy. She was happy to be a "little brush" chosen by Jesus "in order to paint His own image on the souls . . . entrusted to [her] care."[6] How freeing it was not to have to trouble oneself about results or visible successes. It was enough to know that one had done one's best to do God's will and that one could and should leave the outcome to him.

The work of evangelization excels when we let God's light radiate through the limits of our own and others' uniqueness while being faithful to the communal side of our call. When one lives in total commitment to Christ, one can witness to his redemptive love in a gloomy prison as well as in a gothic cathedral. As Thérèse concludes: "Ah! It is prayer, it is sacrifice which give me all my strength; these are the invincible weapons which Jesus has given me."[7] Prompted by this powerful message, we may be less afraid to step into the battlefield of vice versus virtue. We may decide, without wasting another moment, that now is the time to move from a fragmented, fearful existence to a courageous life centered in Christ. Such a life balances gentleness and firmness, self-giving love and dedicated service. A spiritual child is not his or her own person but an epiphany of the Lord. On the verge of death, Thérèse reached the high point of her apostolic deeds: "I felt that God was very close, and that without realizing it, I had spoken words, as does a child, which come not from me but from Him."[8] This intimacy proved to be her finest legacy since:

> Dying of love is what I hope for.
> When I shall see my bonds broken,
> My God will be my Great Reward.
> I don't desire to possess other goods.
> I want to be set on fire with his Love.
> I want to see Him, to unite myself to Him forever.
> That is my Heaven . . . that is my destiny:
> Living on Love!!! . . .[9]

Twelfth Facet of the New Evangelization

To show in all that we say and do the lasting fruits of a ministry lived in, with, and through Christ in fidelity to our call and in commitment to the Church.

Questions for Reflection

1. Wherever you are and in whatever you do, do you pursue with courage the ways in which Jesus wants you to witness to his love, peace, and joy?

2. Does this "mystical martyrdom of love" inspire in you the willingness and readiness to give your all for Jesus, even if you do not always understand what he asks of you?

3. Can you enter into the wonder and work of evangelization without being pulled hither and yon by your fears and misgivings? What inspires this sense of permanent commitment in you?

Closing Prayer

Lord, teach me to listen to your words with childlike wonder without always having to calculate their outcomes. Let me pay attention to more than my analytical mind can grasp. Breathe into me the wisdom that prompts me to witness to your words despite any opposition I may incur. Provide the evangelizing tools I need to turn tiny sparks of love into flames of desire to serve you and your Bride, the Church. When I feel weak and unworthy of so great a commission, bolster my courage to fulfill the apostolic deeds you have so graciously assigned to me. Amen.

Afterword

Evangelization is a timeless challenge; its lasting appeal rests in the simple truth that our lives from start to finish are meant to be one act of love. This grace yields blessings that far outweigh any cross God may ask us to carry. Here again, in a few fresh words, are the twelve facets of evangelical excellence found in this book:

1. Learn to love the hidden life.
2. Appreciate what a treasure the ordinary is.
3. Trust in Divine Mercy as little children do.
4. Receive the sacraments devoutly day after day.
5. Abandon yourself to Father, Son, and Holy Spirit.
6. Foster friendship with God and others.
7. Take up your cross and follow Jesus.
8. Pray unceasingly.
9. Simplify your life.
10. Let God free you to be your best self.
11. Commit yourself—body, mind, and spirit—to living the Gospel.
12. Leave a legacy of evangelical virtues others want to cultivate.

In silence and in spoken words, we are meant to be messengers of the mystery, seeing in every obstacle strewn on our path an opening to becoming more like Jesus. We must be willing to learn from our mistakes and to discern what of God's guidance is in them. Lofty speculations about what it means to proclaim, to worship, and to witness to the Gospel may have to give way to the commitment to live day by day in the most humane way possible. It was not Thérèse's destiny nor may it be ours to enter the ranks of learned theologians, but each day we can add one page to the book of life written on our heart by Jesus Christ. We can abide by the formative truths and practices inherent in the teachings of the Church and follow them faithfully. We can listen with the ears of our inmost being to the directives Jesus gives us through the power of the Holy Spirit, saying with Thérèse, "DRAW ME, WE SHALL RUN."[1]

With the help of the Paraclete, we may succeed occasionally in crossing the boundary between the hidden life of Jesus of Nazareth and its embodiment in the little way of spiritual childhood. What remains to be expressed about this bridge from contemplation to action will be disclosed by those who come after us. We must be content to be ambassadors for Christ called to convey now and to the next generation the deep truths of the Gospel that touch and transform every heart open to them.

God chose Thérèse to be a channel to convey to the Church and to the world how good it is to discover that weakness is not a curse but a blessing; that suffering is not an exit sign but an entrance to pure joy. To die with Christ is to rise with him. This is the paschal mystery that founds our faith and at the same time confounds our ability to describe adequately what awaits us at the threshold between time and eternity. To each of us in closing it is as if Thérèse says: Carry on. Keep courage. Believe in what is yet to come and pray daily: "May Your will be done in me perfectly, and may I arrive at the place You have prepared for me."[2] Amen.

Appendix

Thérèse in Her Own Words

1.

"So I'm a little rascal who is always laughing" (April 4, 1877, to Louise Magdelaine). [1]

2.

"I'm coming to ask you to pray to little Jesus for me because I have many faults and want to correct them . . . so many holes, so many pegs! But with me it's even worse. So I want to correct myself, and, into each little hole, put a pretty little flower which I'll offer to little Jesus to prepare myself for my First Communion" (December 1882, to Mother Marie de Gonzague). [2]

3.

"Every day, I try to perform as many practices as I can, and I do all in my power not to let a single occasion pass by. I am saying at the bottom of my heart the little prayers which form the perfume of roses, as often as I can" (March 1, 1884, to Sister Agnes of Jesus). [3]

4.

"Oh! dear Pauline, I can't tell you today all the things that fill my heart. I can't get my thoughts together. In spite of everything, I feel that I am filled with courage; I am sure God is not going to abandon me. . . . Oh, I want to refuse Him *nothing*, and even though I feel sad and alone on this earth, He still remains with me. And has not St. Teresa said: 'God alone suffices'" (October 8, 1887, to Sister Agnes of Jesus).[4]

5.

"All the distractions of my trip to Rome, the beautiful things that I admired, all of these could not chase from my mind for a single moment the ardent desire that I have to unite myself to Jesus" (December 16, 1887, to Monseigneur Hugonin).[5]

6.

"I desire only one thing when I am in Carmel, it is always (to preserve my place) to suffer for Jesus. Life passes so quickly that truly it must be better to have a very beautiful crown and a little trouble than (not) to have an ordinary one without any trouble and then for a suffering borne without joy, when I think that for all eternity I shall love God better. Then in suffering, one can save souls. Ah, Pauline, if during my life I could have suffered to offer one soul to God, one soul that would be snatched from the fire of hell, oh! how happy I would be" (March 10, 1888, to Sister Agnes of Jesus).[6]

7.

"A day of a Carmelite spent without suffering is a day lost" (May 8, 1888, to Céline).[7]

8.

"It is true that sometimes, for a few moments, we look with scorn at gathering our treasures, and this is the difficult moment. We are tempted to leave all behind, but in one act of love, even *unfelt* love, all is repaired, and Jesus smiles. He is helping us without seeming to do so, and the tears that the wicked make Him shed are dried by our poor and feeble love. Love can do all things, and the most difficult things don't appear difficult to it! Jesus does not look so much at the grandeur of actions or even their difficulty as the love which goes to make up these actions . . ." (October 20, 1888, to Céline).[8]

9.

"Oh! I do not want Jesus to have any sorrow. On the day of my espousals, I would like to convert *all* the sinners of this earth and to save all the souls in purgatory! . . . The Lamb of Jesus is going to laugh when it sees this desire of the little *grain* of sand! . . . I know that it is folly, but, nevertheless, I would like it to be this way so that Jesus has not one single tear to shed" (January 6, 1889, to Sister Agnes of Jesus).[9]

10.

"Life is only a *dream*, and soon we shall wake up, and what joy . . . the greater our sufferings are the more infinite will be our glory. . . . Oh, let us not lose the trial that Jesus is sending us, it is a gold mine to be exploited. Are we going to miss the chance? . . . The grain of sand wants to get to work, without *joy*, without *courage*, without *strength*, and it is all these titles which will facilitate the enterprise for it; it wants to work through love" (February 28, 1889, to Céline).[10]

11.

"Before dying by the sword, let us die by pinpricks . . ." (March 15, 1889, to Céline).[11]

12.

"Let us profit from our one moment of suffering! . . . Let us see only each moment! . . . A moment is a treasure . . . one act of love will make us know Jesus better . . . it will bring us closer to Him during the whole of *eternity*!" (April 26, 1889, to Céline).[12]

13.

"Unknown martyrdom, known to God alone, which the eye of the creature cannot discover, a martyrdom without honor, without triumph. . . . That is love pushed to the point of heroism. . . . But one day, a grateful God will cry out: 'Now my turn.' Oh, what will we see then? What is this life which will no more have an end? . . . God will be the soul of our soul . . . unfathomable mystery. . . . And all this will come *soon*, yes soon" (July 14, 1889, to Céline).[13]

14.

"*Silence*, this is the language that alone can tell you what is happening in my soul!" (May 10, 1890, to Sister Agnes of Jesus).[14]

15.

"Winter is suffering; suffering misunderstood, misjudged, looked upon as useless by profane eyes, but as fruitful and powerful in the eyes of Jesus and the angels who, like the vigilant bees, know how to gather the honey contained within the mysterious and multiple calyxes that represent souls or rather the children of the virginal little flower . . . we must let the bees draw out all the honey from the little calyxes, keeping nothing, giving all to Jesus . . ."(October 20, 1891, to Céline).[15]

16.

"Céline, what a mystery is our grandeur in Jesus. . . . This is all that Jesus has shown us in making us climb the symbolic tree. . . . Let us listen to what he is saying to us. . . .' The foxes have their lairs, the birds of heaven their nests, but I have no place to lay my head.' This is where we must descend in order that we may serve as an abode for Jesus" (October 19, 1892, to Céline).[16]

17.

"I have experienced it; when I *am feeling* nothing, when I am INCAPABLE *of praying*, or practicing virtue, then is the moment for seeking opportunities, *nothings*, which please Jesus more than mastery of the world, or even martyrdom suffered with generosity. For example, a smile, a friendly word, when I would want to say nothing, or put on a look of annoyance, etc., etc." (July 18, 1893, to Céline).[17]

18.

"The wind of sorrow that pushes it (your boat) is the *wind of love*, and this wind is swifter than lightning . . ." (July 23, 1893, to Celine).[18]

19.

"This thought of the brevity of life gives me courage, it helps me bear with the weariness of the road . . . Jesus has gone before us to prepare a place in the home of His Father, and then He will come and He will take us with Him so that where He is we also may be. . . . Let us wait, let us suffer in peace, the hour of rest is approaching, the light tribulations of this life of a moment are preparing us for an eternal weight of glory . . ." (January 1895, to Sister Thérèse-Dosithée (Léonie).[19]

20.

"What does it matter if I appear poor and destitute of mind and talents? . . . I want to put into practice this counsel from the *Imitation*: 'Let this one take glory in one thing, another in something else, but as for you, set your joy only in *contempt of self*, in My Will and my Glory.' Or: 'Do you want to learn something that will help you: Love to be unknown and counted as nothing!' . . . When thinking this over, I felt a great peace in my soul, I felt that here is *truth* and *peace*" (April 28, 1895, to Sister Thérèse-Dosithée (Léonie).[20]

21.

"The science of Love, oh! yes, this word resounds sweetly in the ear of my soul. I desire only this science. Having given all my riches for it, I look upon this as having given nothing. . . . I understand so well that it is only love that can make us pleasing to God, that this love is the only good that I ambition. . . . Ah! If all weak and imperfect souls felt what the littlest of all souls feels, the soul of your little Thérèse, not one would despair of reaching the summit of the mountain of love, since Jesus does not ask for great actions but only abandonment and gratitude . . ." (September 13, 1896, to Sister Marie of the Sacred Heart).[21]

22.

"If the night frightens the little child, if she complains at *not seeing* Him who is carrying her, let her *close her eyes*, let her WILLINGLY make the sacrifice that is asked of her, and then let her await sleep. . . . When she keeps herself peaceful in this way, the night which she is no longer looking at will be unable to frighten her, and soon calm, if not joy, will be reborn in her little heart" (December 1896, to Sister Marie of Saint-Joseph).[22]

23.

"You want to know if I am joyful at going to paradise? I would be very much so *if* I were going there, but . . . I do not count on the illness, it is too slow a leader. *I count only on love.* Ask Good Jesus that all the prayers being offered for me may serve to increase the Fire which must consume me . . ." (June 6, 1897, to Sister Marie of the Trinity).[23]

24.

"I am ascending to heaven . . . I am touching the homeland, I am carrying off the victory! . . . I am about to enter into the abode of the elect, to see beauties that the eye of man has never seen, to listen to harmonies the ear has never heard, to enjoy delights the heart has never tasted. . . . Here I am, brought to the hour which each of us has so much desired! It is very true that the Lord chooses the little ones to confound the great ones of this world. . . . I am a springtime flower that the Master of the garden is plucking for his pleasure. . . . I, a little short-lived creature, am going there first. One day we shall find one another again in Paradise, and we shall enjoy true happiness!" (June 1897, to Mother Agnes of Jesus (Pauline), Sister Marie of the Sacred Heart (Louise), and Sister Genevieve (Céline), her sisters).[24]

Notes

Introduction: The Two Childhoods of Thérèse of Lisieux

1. *The Poetry of St. Thérèse of Lisieux*, trans. Donald Kinney, O.C.D. (Washington, DC: ICS Publications, 1995), 238.
2. *Story of a Soul: The Autobiography of St. Thérèse of Lisieux*, trans. John Clarke, O.C.D. (Washington, DC: ICS Publications, 1975), 238.
3. Ibid., 194.
4. *The Poetry of St. Thérèse of Lisieux*, 142.
5. *Story of a Soul*, 188.
6. Ibid., 195.
7. Ibid., 276.
8. Ibid., 249.

1. The Little Way of Hiddenness

1. *The Poetry of St. Thérèse of Lisieux*, 52.
2. *Story of a Soul*, 58.
3. Ibid., 72.
4. Ibid., 159.
5. Ibid., 249.
6. Ibid., 196.
7. *The Poetry of St. Thérèse of Lisieux*, 203–4.

2. The Little Way of Gratitude

1. *The Poetry of St. Thérèse of Lisieux*, 58.
2. *Story of a Soul*, 159.
3. Ibid., 151.
4. Ibid., 179.
5. Ibid., 14.

3. The Little Way of Trust in Divine Mercy

1. *The Poetry of St. Thérèse of Lisieux*, 126.
2. *Story of a Soul*, 159.
3. Ibid., 208.
4. *The Prayers of St. Thérèse of Lisieux*, trans. Aletheia Kane, O.C.D. (Washington, DC: ICS Publications, 1997), 116.
5. *Story of a Soul*, 58.
6. Ibid., 47.

4. The Little Way of Sacramental Life

1. *The Poetry of St. Thérèse of Lisieux*, 112.
2. *Story of a Soul*, 143.
3. Ibid., 147.

4.   Ibid., 228.
5.   Ibid., 229.
6.   Ibid.
7.   Ibid., 112.
8.   Ibid., 80.
9.   Ibid.
10. Ibid., 40.
11. Ibid., 76.
12. Ibid., 149.
13. Ibid.
14. Ibid., 77.
15. Ibid., 263.
16. Ibid., 173.
17. Ibid.
18. Ibid., 221.
19. Ibid., 263, author's italics.

5. The Little Way of Abandonment to Divine Providence
1.   *The Poetry of St. Thérèse of Lisieux*, 79.
2.   *Story of a Soul*, 176.
3.   Ibid., 178.
4.   Ibid., 220.
5.   *The Collected Letters of St. Thérèse of Lisieux, Volumes I and II*, trans. F. J. Sheed (London: Sheed & Ward, 1972), 275.
6.   *Story of a Soul*, 271.
7.   Ibid., 242.

6. The Little Way of Experiencing Friendship with God and Others
1.   *The Poetry of St. Thérèse of Lisieux*, 83.
2.   *Story of a Soul*, 143.
3.   Ibid., 157.
4.   Ibid., 189.
5.   Ibid.
6.   Ibid., 235.

7. The Little Way of Renunciation
1.   *The Poetry of St. Thérèse of Lisieux*, 92.
2.   *Story of a Soul*, 77.
3.   Ibid., 249–50.
4.   Ibid., 179.
5.   Ibid., 188.
6.   Ibid., 198.
7.   Ibid., 79.
8.   Ibid., 199.

8. The Little Way of Unceasing, World-Redeeming Prayer

1. *The Poetry of St. Thérèse of Lisieux*, 130.
2. *Story of a Soul*, 192.
3. Ibid.
4. Ibid., 192–93.
5. Ibid., 193.
6. Ibid.
7. Ibid., 195.
8. Ibid., 258–59.
9. Ibid., 242.
10. Ibid., 239.

9. The Little Way of Simplicity

1. *The Poetry of St. Thérèse of Lisieux*, 77.
2. *Story of a Soul*, 14.
3. Ibid., 151.
4. Ibid., 233.

10. The Little Way of Freedom

1. *The Poetry of St. Thérèse of Lisieux*, 55.
2. *Story of a Soul*, 179.
3. "Sayings of Light and Love" in *The Collected Works of St. John of the Cross*, trans. Kieran Kavanagh and Otilio Rodriguez (Washington, DC: ICS Publications, 1992), no. 28.
4. Ibid., no. 55.
5. Ibid., no. 16.
6. Ibid., no. 60.
7. *Story of a Soul*, 277.
8. Ibid., 270.

11. The Little Way of Purgation, Illumination, and Union

1. *The Poetry of St. Thérèse of Lisieux*, 134–35.
2. *Story of a Soul*, 190.
3. Ibid., 151–52.
4. Ibid., 218.
5. Ibid., 235.
6. Ibid.
7. Ibid., 214.
8. *Poetry of St. Thérèse of Lisieux*, 43.

12. The Little Way of Living in, with, and through the Lord in a Mystical Martyrdom of Love

1. *The Poetry of St. Thérèse of Lisieux*, 83.
2. *Story of a Soul*, 165.
3. Ibid., 214.

4. Ibid., 218.
5. Ibid., 233.
6. Ibid., 235.
7. Ibid., 241.
8. Ibid., 243.
9. *Poetry of St. Thérèse of Lisieux*, 92.

Afterword
1. *Story of a Soul*, 254.
2. Ibid., 275.

Appendix: Thérèse in Her Own Words
1. *Letters of St. Thérèse of Lisieux*, Volume I, 1877–1890, trans. John Clarke, O.C.D. (Washington, DC: ICS Publications, 1982), 110.
2. Ibid., 152.
3. Ibid., 190.
4. Ibid., 289.
5. Ibid., 387.
6. Ibid., 399.
7. Ibid., 423.
8. Ibid., 467–68.
9. Ibid., 500.
10. Ibid., 537.
11. Ibid., 552.
12. Ibid., 558.
13. Ibid., 577.
14. Ibid., 620.
15. *Letters of St. Thérèse of Lisieux*, Volume II, 1890–1897, trans. John Clarke, O.C.D. (Washington, DC: ICS Publications, 1988), 741.
16. Ibid., 761.
17. Ibid., 801.
18. Ibid., 804.
19. Ibid., 896.
20. Ibid., 902–03.
21. Ibid., 994.
22. Ibid., 1033.
23. Ibid., 1120–21.
24. Ibid., 1129.

For Further Reading

Ahern, Patrick. *Maurice and Thérèse: The Story of a Love*. New York: Doubleday, 1998.

à Kempis, Thomas. *The Imitation of Christ*. Edited by Harold C. Gardiner. Garden City, NY: Image Books, 1955.

Bouyer, Louis. *Introduction to Spirituality*. Translated by Mary Perkins Ryan. New York: Desclée, 1961.

———. *Women Mystics*. Translated by Anne England Nash. San Francisco: Ignatius Press, 1993.

Boylan, Dom Eugene. *This Tremendous Lover*. Paramus, NJ: Newman Press, 1964.

Brother Lawrence of the Resurrection. *The Practice of the Presence of God*. Translated by Salvatore Sciuba. Washington, DC: ICS Publications, 1994.

Carey, Terence, O.C.D., ed. *Thérèse of Lisieux: A Discovery of Love*. Hyde Park, NY: New City Press, 1992.

Caussade, Jean-Pierre de. *Abandonment to Divine Providence*. Translated by John Beevers. Garden City, NY: Image Books, 1975.

D'Elbee, Jean C. J. Father, *I Believe in Love: A Personal Retreat Based on the Teaching of St. Thérèse of Lisieux*. Manchester, NH: Sophia Institute Press, 1974.

de les Gavarres, Angel. *Thérèse, The Little Child of God's Mercy* (Her Spiritual Itinerary in the Light of Her Autobiographical Manuscripts, Washington, DC: ICS Publications, 1999.

de Sales, Francis. *Introduction to the Devout Life*. Translated by Michael Day. New York: E. P. Dutton, 1961.

Foley, Marc, O.C.D. *The Context of Holiness: Psychological and Spiritual Reflections on the Life of St. Thérèse of Lisieux*. Washington, DC: ICS Publications, 2008.

Frost, Maurice. *St. Thérèse of Lisieux and the World: An Encounter*. Dublin, Ireland: The Theresian Trust, 1997.

Gaucher, Guy. *The Passion of Thérèse of Lisieux*. New York: Crossroad, 2006.

Jamart, Francois. *Complete Spiritual Doctrine of St. Thérèse of Lisieux*. Translated by Walter van de Putte. New York: St. Paul Publications, 1961.

Muto, Susan. *Blessings that Make Us Be: A Formative Approach to Living the Beatitudes*. Pittsburgh, PA: Epiphany Books, 2002.

————. *John of the Cross for Today: The Ascent.* Pittsburgh, PA: Epiphany Books, 1998.

————. *John of the Cross for Today: The Dark Night.* Pittsburgh, PA: Epiphany Books, 2000.

————. "One Act of Love" (First Installment). *Carmelite Digest,* Fall, 2008: 68–79.

————. "One Act of Love" (Second Installment), *Carmelite Digest,* Winter, 2008: 69–79.

————. "One Act of Love" (Third Installment), *Carmelite Digest,* Spring, 2009: 25–37.

————. *A Practical Guide to Spiritual Reading.* Petersham, MA: St. Bede's Publications, 1994.

————. *Steps Along the Way: The Path of Spiritual Reading.* Denville, NJ: Dimension Books, 1975.

————. *The Journey Homeward: On the Road of Spiritual Reading.* Denville, NJ: Dimension Books, 1977.

————. *Virtues: Your Christian Legacy.* Steubenville, OH: Emmaus Road, 2014.

————. *Words of Wisdom for Our World: The Precautions and Counsels of St. John of the Cross.* Eugene, OR: Wipf and Stock, 2009.

Petit, Jean. *Descending Fire: The Journal of a Soul Aflame.* Manchester, NH: Sophia Institute Press, 1953.

Piat, Stephane-Joseph, O.F.M. *Celine: Sister Genevieve of the Holy Face.* Sister and Witness of Saint Thérèse of the Child Jesus. San Francisco: Ignatius Press, 1997.

The Poetry of Saint Thérèse of Lisieux. Translated by Donald Kinney, O.C.D. Washington, DC: ICS Publications, 1996.

The Prayers of Saint Thérèse of Lisieux. Translated by Aletheia Kane, O.C.D. Washington, DC: ICS Publications, 1997.

Rego, Aloysius, "The Book of the Gospels Never Leaves Me: Reading the Scriptures with St. Thérèse." *Mount Carmel.* Volume 60, Number 4. October-December 2012, 17–23.

The Sayings of Light and Love in The Collected Works of St. John of the Cross. Translated by Kieran Kavanaugh, O.C.D. and Otilio Rodriguez, O.C.D. Washington, DC: ICS Publications, 1991.

Schmidt, Joseph F. *Everything Is Grace: The Life and Way of Thérèse of Lisieux.* Frederick, MD: The Word Among Us Press, 2007.

Scholtes, Marinus. *Become Jesus: The Diary of a Soul Touched by God.* trans. Joop Bekkers, Ph.D. Edited with an Introduction and

Afterword by Adrian van Kaam and Susan Muto. Pittsburgh, PA: Epiphany Books, 1998.

Stinissen, Wilfred. *Into Your Hands, Father: Abandoning Ourselves to the God Who Loves Us*. San Francisco: Ignatius Press, 2011.

Tanquerey, Adolphe. *The Spiritual Life: A Treatise on Ascetical and Mystical Theology*. Translated by Herman Branderis. Westminster, MD: Christian Classics, 1930.

Teresa of Ávila, The Book of Her Life in The Collected Works. Vol. One, Translated by Kieran Kavanaugh, and Otilio Rodriguez. Washington, DC: ICS Publications. 1980.

Thérèse of Lisieux. *Her Last Conversations*. Translated by John Clarke, O.C.D. Washing, DC: ICS Publications, 1977.

———. *Letters of St. Thérèse of Lisieux*. Volume I, 1877–1890. Translated by John Clarke, Washington, DC: ICS Publications, 1982.

———. *Letters of St. Thérèse of Lisieux*. Volume II, 1890–1897. Translated by John Clarke, Washington, DC: ICS Publications, 1988.

———. *The Autobiography of St. Thérèse of Lisieux: Story of a Soul*. Translated by John Clarke, O.C.D. Washington, DC: ICS Publications. 1975.

Underhill, Evelyn. *Mysticism*. New York: E. P. Dutton, 1961.

van Kaam, Adrian. *The Life Story of a Joyful Man of God: The Autobiographical Memoirs of Adrian van Kaam*. Edited by Susan Muto, Eugene, OR: Wipf & Stock, 2010.

———. *The Music of Eternity: Everyday Sound of Fidelity*. Pittsburgh, PA: Epiphany Books, 2001.

———. *The Transcendent Self: Formative Spirituality of the Middle, Early and Later Years of Life*. Pittsburgh, PA: Epiphany Association, 1991.

van Kaam, Adrian and Susan Muto. *Formation of the Christian Heart* Formation Theology Series. Volume Three. Pittsburgh, PA: Epiphany Books, 2006.

———. *Living Our Christian Faith and Formation Traditions*. Formation Theology Series. Volume Four. Pittsburgh, PA: Epiphany Books, 2007.

———. *The Power of Appreciation: A New Approach to Personal and Relational Healing*. Pittsburgh, PA: Epiphany Books, 1999.

von Balthasar, Hans Urs. *Two Sisters in the Spirit: Thérèse of Lisieux and Elizabeth of the Trinity*. San Francisco: Ignatius Press, 1992.

Susan Muto, executive director of the Epiphany Association, is a renowned speaker, author, teacher, and is dean of the Epiphany Academy of Formative Spirituality.

Muto earned a master's degree and a doctorate in English literature from the University of Pittsburgh, where she specialized in the work of post-Reformation spiritual writers. Beginning in 1966, she served in administrative positions at the Institute of Formative Spirituality at Duquesne University and taught as a full professor in its programs, edited its journals, and served as its director from 1981 to 1988.

Muto is a frequent contributor to scholarly and popular journals such as *Mount Carmel* and *Spiritual Life Magazine*, and served as editor of Epiphany's online journals and courses, including *Growing in, with, and through Christ*. She is the author of more than thirty books, among them *Table of Plenty*, *Then God Said*, and *Virtues: Your Christian Legacy*. She is the coauthor—with Rev. Adrian van Kaam, C.S.Sp. (1920–2007)—of more than forty books, including *Commitment: Key to Christian Maturity*, and *The Power of Appreciation*.

Muto lectures and leads conferences, seminars, workshops, and institutes nationally and internationally. She has received many distinctions for her work, including a doctor of humanities degree from King's College, Wilkes-Barre, Pennsylvania. She was one of four Catholic writers to be honored in 2009 with a lifetime achievement award by the Catholic Historical Society of Western Pennsylvania. Muto also is the recipient of the 2014 Aggiornamento Award presented of the Catholic Library Association. She lives in Pittsburgh, Pennsylvania.